GOD-

FAITH

Discovering the pure logic built into the fabric of reality

Jeff Grupp

PLC Books Kalamazoo

GOD-
FAITH

Discovering the pure logic built into the fabric of reality

PLC Books Kalamazoo (Kalamazoo Michigan)

GOD-FAITH

2 Corinthians 4:18 King James Version (KJV)

18 While we look not at the things which are seen, but at the things which are not seen: for the things which are seen are temporal; but the things which are not seen are eternal.

2 Corinthians 10:5 New International Version (NIV)

We demolish arguments and every pretension that sets itself up against the knowledge of God, and we take captive every thought to make it obedient to Christ.

Isaiah 61:10 New International Version (NIV)

10 I delight greatly in the Lord; my soul rejoices in my God. For he has clothed me with garments of salvation and arrayed me in a robe of his righteousness...

Hebrews 11:6 New International Reader's Version (NIRV)

6 Without faith it is impossible to please God. Those who come to God must believe that he exists. And they must believe that he rewards those who look to him.

Ecclesiastes 11:5 (NRSV)

5 Just as you do not know how the breath comes to the bones in the mother's womb, so you do not know the work of God, who makes everything.

Galatians 2:20 English Standard Version (ESV)

20 I have been crucified with Christ. It is no longer I who live, but Christ who lives in me. And the life I now live in the flesh I live by faith in the Son of God, who loved me and gave himself for me.

Psalm 73:24-25 English Standard Version (ESV)

24 You guide me with your counsel, and afterward you will receive me to glory. 25 Whom have I in heaven but you? And there is nothing on earth that I desire besides you.

Contents

PART 0: Pure Logic Discloses that Ultimate Reality is a Biblical-Christian Ontology

This book is meant to be a breakthrough in theology and ministry, truly answering, with new information and logical findings, the major cruxes of theology that have persisted over the past centuries (for example, why God would create, and/or not fix, a world that has pain). Also, I will specifically show, with simple reason and pure logic, that if anything whatsoever exists, _the only logical option is that it is created by the Christian God_. In undertaking this, I will present a new proof for the existence of the Christian God of the Bible, which has as its starting point the most certain knowledge there is, Descartes' famous inference, "I think therefore I am". For that reason, this new argument for the existence of the Christian God starts right where it should: in what is most certainly known to exist. I will merely start at that point, and move forward through chapters 1 – 4 to arrive at this new and surprisingly simple proof for the existence of the God of the Bible. It is a _logical_ proof, but has its base in and from the certainty of "I think therefore I am". In other words, the argument's impetus could _not_ be more certain, and thus the simple steps that follow from the impetus, lead to logical deductions that one can be entirely confident in, in leading to inference and proof for the existence of the Christian God. Along the way, the argumentation in this book, in Chapter 2, will definitively solve the long-standing *problem of evil,* with a new proof hitherto undiscussed, to my knowledge. Of perhaps the most importance is that after starting from "I think therefore I am", I only use the simplest of pure logical principles to come to the conclusions of this book. So, this book is, in a sense, is a pure logic textbook about ultimate and universal reality, which means, as we will also see, that the Bible is the purest logic textbook, the ultimate book about the deductive logic of reality, the engineering schematic for reality-as-a-whole. The logic of reality, uncovered in this book, has not been hidden, but rather people have just not seen it: "For God speaks again and again, though people do not recognize it" (Job 33:13 NLT).

This book should be especially relevant to atheists, professional academics, practitioners of Eastern religion, religious but non-Christian persons, occultists and satanists, and those who are of the belief that logic and science disprove the existence of the Christian God. This book is most relevant to either Christians who are struggling with, or non-Christians who are put-off by, the Bible and Christianity due to not knowing satisfactory answers to the following sorts of questions:

- How can it be that a perfect and loving God created a universe with so much pain and evil?
- How do we know there is a God at all?
- Which religion is right? How do we know—I mean *really know*, without fudging the issue—that the Christian God is the true One?

- Why is the Old Testament so strange? Why would God say, "do not kill," and then command all sorts of murders?

- Why does God feel distant? Why can't I see God, or have powerful experience of His presence? How can I experience God to the fullest, living from His power and presence, all the time, hiding away in Him always, so that I always have everything I need?

- Why hasn't science found any evidence for God? I know many say science *has*, but if that's true, why aren't all convinced who see this supposed scientific evidence, if there is any?[1]

To summarize this book in different words: starting with the most certain experience and information a person can have (which is that I am an experiencing self: I am an *I am*), I will find that the simplest and most basic logical analysis of reality, leads *from* the *I am*, *to* reality as-a-whole being thoroughly describable by an uncomplicated and starkly beautiful, elegant, and logical Christian-Biblical axiomatic. So, in other words,

> *Pure logic, derived from the most certain rudiments of mind-experience (that there is an I am), reveals an elemental knowledge of the mechanics of reality as having a Christian ontology built into the logical texture of reality.*

If one investigates *into* the reality of what is truly known, penetrating into the reality of things that are known with certainty to exist (such as the *I am*), rather than investigating what is *not* known with certainty, analysis

---

[1] For additional questions such as, Why is there a Hell? And Why would there be a doctrine of predestination? See my previous book, *Theologic* (2018).

penetrating into certain and known reality directly and immediately reveals its monotheistic and omnipresent Creator (the divine Logos).

These arguments arose from my own inability to answer the questions in the bulleted list on the previous page to inmates in the jail that I am a preacher and chaplain at. I prayed to God for simple, clear, illuminating, answers to these and other similar questions, to be shown the simple truth about them, and answers that could be used in the ministry setting. This book is an account of the answers I received.

Just before putting this book out for publication, I was having breakfast with a pastor friend of mine, discussing the simple argument in Chapter 2, for why God would create a universe that involves so much pain and evil, and we were both, I think it's safe to say, calmly amazed at the simplicity and finality of which the argument presented in that chapter *gets the job done* in answering that long-unanswered question. The arguments and basic logic in this book show that built into the very fabric of reality—or of *any* reality whatsoever that can exist—is pure, unavoidable *dependence* for its being on the Christian creator-God. The logic is, I think it's safe to say, astonishingly simple, and the discoveries of Chapter 4, for example—which show (to give just one example) that if any reality exists, it can only be the creation of a creator-God of infinite sacrificial love (that is, the God of the Bible)—are, in my opinion, drop-to-your-knees breakthroughs.

The three parts of this book are, to some degree, stand-alone sections, and need not be read in order. Also, I rely heavily on the use the simple device of *logical arguments*. Briefly put, a logical argument consists of a set of data points, called premises, that contain terse bits of evidence, where the premises, or data, is then combined to "spit-out" a specific conclusion. To give a specific example, when I was teaching logic and critical thinking at the University of Michigan - Dearborn, I would, interestingly, demonstrate what an argument was on the first day of class by showing the students the following argument, which I did not, at the time, necessarily intend to be taken completely seriously, but rather was to just demonstrate the force of how the data points to (infers to) the conclusion in a logical argument (but I did not know how relevant the argument really was at the time):

1. Consciousness is non-physical.
2. Non-physical things are supernatural.
3. You are composed of consciousness.
4. Conclusion: You are supernatural.

The premises (the data) make an inference to the conclusion. The main points of the book, for the most part, are presented in logical argument form.

Part 2 has two primary objectives: (1) to show that the hugely popular and seemingly intellectual philosophy of atheism that is spreading in popularity across the world is internally contradictory, and (2) to begin to establish a _Biblical_ definition of what _faith_ is. (2) may seem rather bland, but this is an incredibly misunderstood and spiritually contemplative topic, and it is also a prelude to Part 3, which is largely about Christian meditation and experiencing God. The Biblical definition of faith has been investigated by astonishingly few in the atheist or theist camps, and when this definition is discovered carefully from Scripture, by using the verses that are translated with the word "faith" in them, they show that Biblical faith amounts to being a description of a channel of information or presence, for lack of better words, _from_ God _to_ salvific and potentially salvific people, _implanted into_ people by God, from moment-to-moment, leading to explosive wisdom, prophetic knowledge, direct awareness of God, and other spiritual gifts. This analysis of the definition of Biblical faith is revealed to be a far more experience-oriented, meditation-oriented, trans-scientific, system of direct communion with Jesus.

PART 1: If Anything Exists, It Can Only Be a Creation of the God of the Bible

1. The Man-is-a-Spirit Argument for the Existence of God

Why Does My Mind Look Like a Nonphysical Spirit, if Professional Academics Tell Me It's Just a Brain-State?

In this chapter I will present a proof that is directly verifiable for any human being, that proves the existence of a creator-God. I call the argument *the man-is-a-spirit argument for the existence of God*, and the argument is as follows:

1. When doing introspection, I can see that my thoughts, my feelings, my mind, are viewed to be *nonphysical*, and resemble a spirit, not a matter-brain or brain-state.

2. Only a spirit can cause/create a spirit to exist.

3. <u>Conclusion</u>: I am created by a spirit, rather than by a natural process from external reality.[2,3]

---

[2] I believe this argument would fit into being roughly a form of the so-called *argument from consciousness*, which is alleged to prove the existence of God. I am going about this argument from a rather different approach than how the argument from consciousness is usually approached, however. The argument from consciousness has the following standard form, as the form given below, and from the popular atheist website, infidels.org (https://infidels.org/library/modern/steven_conifer/ac.html, Section II):

    (A) It is a fact that human consciousness exists.
    (B) That fact can be adequately explained within a theistic framework (i.e., one which posits God's existence), whereas it cannot be adequately explained within an atheistic (or naturalistic) framework (i.e., one which denies God's existence).
    (C) Hence, there is a fact which only theism can adequately explain.
    (D) Therefore, God must exist.

[3] At the very end of this chapter I present reasoning that would seem to very strongly support the idea that the specific "spirit" referred to in this argument can only be the Christian God of the Bible, and that will be proven in later chapters.

This argument is simple, it would appear to prove that a creator-God _has created you_, and its being anchored in direct experience and simple logic makes the argument seemingly undeniable. The direct experience I am referring to is in premise 1:

1. When doing introspection, I can see that my thoughts, feelings, my mind, are viewed to be _nonphysical_, and resemble a spirit, not a matter-brain or brain-state.

This is not a complicated issue. When you look at yourself within, you don't look at all, in any way, like any sort of physical object: a feeling does not look like a cinder block. Every single person reading this sentence can, right now, verify that this premise is thoroughly accurate. And there is nothing more immediately verifiable than this, and no information is more reliable[4]. Even professional academics who want to deny that the mind is nonphysical will in all but a few cases readily admit that a person's mind _does_ certainly appear nonphysical. But if it does, _then it looks like a spirit_: the definition of a nonphysical being is a spirit, so if the only thing you can verify about your inner self is that you are a nonphysical being, then all you know about yourself is that you are a spirt. So, the question is: Are you, in fact, actually seeing a spirit when you look at yourself? In other words: are you a spirit, rather than a matter-bran, or a central nervous system?[5] Do we trust what we directly see when we look inside at ourselves, or do we trust professional philosophers and academics who demand that, while you certainly _do_ see

---

[4] I say this because when we introspectively view our own minds we are seemingly _directly_ observing mind and mind-contents, rather than _representationally_ observing, as is the case when we perceive external-physical reality outside of our selves. This leads to observation of external reality having far less reliable information than information obtained by introspective observation (to understate the issue). This subject will be explored again in Part 2 of this book.

[5] The Bible contains the thesis that a human is in fact a spirit, by the following reasoning: God is a Spirit (John 4;24), humans resemble God (Elohim) (Gen 1:26, Gen 9:6, James 3:9)

what looks exactly like a nonphysical item when you look inwardly at your mind and its contents, that is, however, some sort of an illusion, and that nonphysical presence, the spectacular mystical *spirit* you directly see, as being your *self within*, is actually, *somehow*, a hunk of meat (a brain, or a brain-state). Which is more reliable information: what you can directly observe for yourself with your own mind's-eye, or what professional academics tell you when they tell you that what you see is not really what it seems to be (a claim they have no evidence for)?

So, there is a strong trend against the sort of reasoning found in the man-is-a-spirit argument, mainly coming from professional academics, who want to prevent its line of reason from starting, by saying there is a problem already at step 1. They tell us that, though we may believe it *seems* that our inner mind, our inner self, appears *as if* it is a nonphysical entity, that is, however, nevertheless, an illusion, and the mind is a physical brain-process, wherein we should not believe we arrive at the conclusion of the above argument. In this chapter, I will show how this objection from professional academics—an objection that is *hugely* popular in the world today—is nonevidential, non-verifiable, and contradictory; and instead, all evidence points to the viewable datum that our inner self is a spirit, and this directly observable fact reveals that a creator-God is real.

Professional academics demand that my consciousness, as *mysterious* as it is (to use Searle's terminology[6]), is no more than an aspect of my brain—all the sheer differentness and total not-matter-like nature of my feelings and thoughts, are just the workings of a hunk of meat in my head (my brain) that became very complex by evolving through eons of time, by unknown

---

[6] Searle, John, 1977, *The Mystery of Consciousness*, New York: New York Review of Books, p. xii.

processes, that were not seen by any human, and which cannot even be described or defined.

But when I look at my inner consciousness and inner self, there is no other object in my reality that I see that looks like _those_. In fact, the properties of my inner self and consciousness are the _opposite_ of the properties of the physical items of the world—which would mean mind and self are nonphysical, and therefore _are like a spirit_, rather than like matter items. That which has physical properties is physical, and that which is devoid of all physical properties is nonphysical. The professional academic does not want to venture into these directly confirmable findings that are obtained by directly looking at mind/consciousness within, and the professional academic wants to study mind/consciousness primarily by studying brain-matter. In other words, the professional academic, in studying consciousness, wants to only study aspects of the body, rather than the viewable spirit within. In no place below will I argue for mind-body dualism, as this book breaks new ground for, and presents new evidence for what I call nonphysical Calvinism (a type of simulation theory), but this book does not side-step that consciousness (mind, self) _is an entity_, and an entity that can be _directly viewed_, and by doing so, the viewer sees something that looks completely different than anything else in reality (it looks like a _spirit_), and this is quite supportive for the claim that a creator-God exists and created your mind-self.

That mind, when one looks right at it, looks like a spirit, and not like a hunk of meat, is perhaps the most revealing and important finding about our existence, as human beings, since it appears to reveal who and what we are, and since it appears to prove where we come from, in proving that a creator-God exists.

Since we do not see any items in physical reality that have an appearance like the nonphysical-looking contents of mind and consciousness, we will see that it can be inferred that the nonphysicality of the mind apparently requires a different cause, origin, and reason for its existence, as compared to physical things like bricks, rocks, clouds, organic matter, worlds, and anything else in physical reality.

Physical properties are, for example, extension (spatial size or magnitude), solidity, colorful surface, motion, to name a few. How can what appears without any physicality be derived only from physicality? And how can what is purely physical cause that which is viewable as being entirely devoid of any physicality? Is this like saying we can derive motion from stillness? Or redness from blueness? How can I not be seeing nonphysical "stuff" inside of me, when I am clearly seeing nonphysical "stuff"? Denying what our self looks like when we introspect would be like saying that when looking deeply into the clear sky, I am not seeing the color *blue that I am witnessing right now* (contradiction).

Why Do Prestigious Academics Tell Us That Mind is Physical?

I recall reading many books back in my 20s and 30s by Dennett, Pinker, and the philosophers of mind who occupied the prestigious academic positions in the United States, with books that had impressive titles, such as *Consciousness Explained*, believing that I'd actually be reading books that contained some solid information for what the apparently nonphysical-looking inner-mind *really was*, how it could be explained scientifically, and why it appeared *as if* it was a spirit, but really *was not*. I recall one day, after weeks of drudging through Stephen Pinker's monstrous book, *How the Mind Works*, having a realization that the book in no way was going to explain to me how the mind *really* works, why I can have inner visual experiences in my consciousness when there was no television screen in my brain, or *what* this inner spirit within me (that *was* me) in fact *was*. And I realized, finally, that Pinker, like Dennett, Searle, and the rest of the of the great philosophers of mind who claimed they could show what the mind really *is* and *why* it is *physical*, in fact could *not* tell me, could not show me, how those things were so—but in fact they had no idea, and their books were not disclosing a revelation on what, who, *I was*—or on what this inwardly viewable spirit-self at the core of my being, in fact truly *was*. Who you are, and what you are, is not disclosed by theories from men, but rather is disclosed by the man-is-a-spirit argument given above, which is directly verifiable by you, and therefore transcends, outstrips, any theories given by any person.

What are the reasons that the professional academic tells us that we are *not* the nonphysical mind directly observe within? It is standard for professional academics, and philosophers of mind, to tell us two things in response to the idea that we believe—or, they say, that we *wrongly believe*—we are directly seeing a nonphysical mind when we introspect in order to look at our inner self:

1. What you think you are seeing (a nonphysical mind) within is not really what you are seeing, it's not what you believe it is, you are witnessing an illusion.

2. Professional academics are making progress in understanding and explaining what mind, inner self, consciousness *is*, in physical terms, and why it *appears* as if it is a nonphysical item when it in fact is not.[7]

Many explanations for these points are given, but it is important to note that, in the end, absolutely no evidence exists for either point. This is important, since professional academics will confidently present information as if they are showing how and why mind is physical, but where it is certainly not the case. For example, consider what the well-known philosopher of mind, Stephen Law, says in response to the idea that mind can be viewed as nonphysical.

> What you are articulating about the mind is an intuition that it just *couldn't* be physical. We need to sharpen that up a bit, because... all we are saying is, "gee, doesn't it *seem* nonphysical. From the inside, this experience I am having... doesn't feel like a brain-state... This is just begging the question... Maybe this experience that I am having now *is* a brain-state, it's just that it doesn't *seem* that way, but that does not mean it *isn't*... Take a glass of water, it doesn't *seem* like a vast collection of ... atoms put together in a particular kind of way, but that's just what it is, appearances are deceptive, and it may be that that's the case in *this* case.[8]

---

[7] Some academics give other "explanations," which are that mind and consciousness does not exist, it is just a property that emerges from brain-meat, that it is only a type of language (but they do not explain how inner thought-sound occurs in thinking of human mental activity), and so forth. All of these cannot explain why I see, within me, picture images, feelings, and I "hear" thought sounds, so I will not discuss these, considering them to be too detached from reality to consider seriously.

[8] "Stephen Law Anything Non physical about the Mind", YouTube, Channel: Galen Orwell, May 7, 2014, https://www.youtube.com/watch?v=JLS1DEhYxns This commentary is from the closertotruth.com series with Robert Lawrence Kuhn. The quote above starts at 3:42 into this YouTube video.

Notice that Law has nothing but a suggestion—no verifiable evidence—that the nonphysical mind is physical, that what one experiences within as mind as nonphysical is *not* a precise and correct observation.

And notice that his comparison about water not looking like atoms, at first glance, *sounds convincing*, but let's look a little further into it—where when we do, we will find it is plainly fallacious to the issue at hand, on multiple levels. Firstly, water *is* a collection of atoms, just like sentences are word-collections in meaningful arrangements, beaches are collections of sand-particles, organisms are organized cell-collections, and populations are ordered people-collections. But the error Law is making is that *those are all objects and systems viewed outside the self, and thus are not comparable to items viewed inside the self*. This is an absolutely central issue, missed by nearly everyone who discusses and analyzes what mind is: when we view inner content, or outer world items, we are looking in contrary directions, and in entirely different places, so it should not be should surprising if the items viewed in either realm were different, or even the opposite of each other, in some regards. The average person has a difficult time believing that mind is nonphysical, even though they can plainly see it within, since they are so accustomed to, and oriented to, *physical* objects *outside* of self. But objects within and those outside of self exist in very different realms—what I mean by that is, If I want to see a physical object outside of myself, I have to look one direction (away from self), and if I want to see subjective content within self, I have to look the opposite (toward and within self). When we look in either of these places, we see entities with different properties, and if we want to understand the big-picture about reality and about who we are, what we are, we have to be honest with ourselves about what we are seeing in either realm, and we have to study either realm and make our conclusions with accurate, sincere, and genuine findings.

As we've discussed, objects outside of self, which are believed to be outside of consciousness and in the world, have entirely different appearances as compared to objects inside of, and/or composing, consciousness: a feeling does not look like a brick. So Law's analogy in comparing water (an object outside of mind) to the appearance that mind (inner) is nonphysical, is like comparing apples and to non-apples, and all that Law is actually discussing is merely an issue of *mereology* (the study of part-whole relationships) of an external object (water), but where the issue of directly observing the inner mind and seeing something that looks like a spirit is in no way primarily a mereological issue, and does not answer the concern we have for:

> *Why am I having a specific experience when I look inside myself, that I am a spirit, and not a physical-brain-state?*

Law is essentially saying the following:

> A person can directly see X, but for no good reason yet suggested, we should not believe the X that we are directly seeing is real.

In the case of Law's context here,

> X = nonphysical consciousness within self.

But we could change X to be about an external world (rather than inner mind) object, and set X = *the sky is blue*, and run the same formula:

> A person can directly see the sky is blue, but for no good reason yet suggested, we should not believe the blueness of the sky that we are directly seeing is real.

Law's comment that water-is-molecules involves the issue that external-physical reality is being perceived incorrectly, in this case seeing water when there are really just molecules, but that comparison does not apply to mind. With water, it is believed that the water it is made up of molecules, but while we can think of water-as-molecules, or sky-as-atoms, according to Law's analogy, the analogous move would be to consider, for example, a feeling-as-_??_ But what is a feeling made of? What are its particles? These questions have no meaning, since a feeling is not known to be reducible to any further constituents. In other words, we have theories about what water and sky are made up of, but not what mind-contents are made up of. The question, _What is a feeling made up of?_, has absolutely no answer, and may even be unanswerable to a human. When we look _out_ at the world, the physical items we experience are theorized and vaguely seen as being composed of tiny particles, but that is not known to also be the case for _inner_ mind-contents, many of which, could very well be, and certainly appear to be, _irreducible_. Mind-contents are not known to break down further (unless mind, or self, as-a-whole or breaks apart completely or loses its realness, convincingness, wherein one sees God "behind" the mind, which we will discuss in Part 3). In addition to the problems in the previous few paragraphs about Law's comment comparing water to nonphysical mind, this would appear to be another fatal problem for Law's analogy comparing water and nonphysical mind.

So, in summing up our comments about Law's commentary,

1) Not seeing that water actually is molecules is an external world perception problem, not an introspecting the inner mind problem

(which does not involve the same problems that external world perception involves).

2) There is no evidence that mind-contents are reducible into smaller pieces, or into particles, like extended physical items are, and therefore, an inwardly viewed feeling, for example, is apparently irreducible, and can't be compared to water being molecules (reductionism): the mereology of water can't be compared to something like a feeling, which appears to be atomic, not mereological. So, in this case, Law is making an analogy between things that have *inverse* properties.

3) Directly viewing inner mind content is not comparable to viewing representational[9] external physical world contents, since the internal and external realms contain different sorts of objects with different sorts of entities, not in any way in a one-to-one comparison.

Law's comments are quite problematical, his analogy is riddled with serious problems. As I was saying above, professional academics will confidently explain their theories for why mind appears nonphysical but is actually a brain state, but when one simply investigates their analysis a bit, their theories for this always fall into absurdity.

To repeat what we were starting to explore at the outset of our discussion about Law's comments, our only point of concern, is that when we look at mind, inwardly, it appears like a spirit. Experiencing a feeling, for example, fills the mind with a nonphysical state, and at that point of feeling (having feeling consciousness, such as experiencing love), the only thing that is

---

[9] We will discuss representationalism in Part 3.

known about mind is that any and everything about it is observed to be *nonphysical*. Inner viewable mind is wholly nonphysical at that moment.

But the same simple reasoning could be said for any content of inner mind. For example, the blueness experience when looking at the sky, regardless if one believes the sky is actually colorless atoms wherein blue-experience is actually erroneous (and wherein the blueness does not represent what the sky actually looks like), or regardless of anything that could be theorized about the sky outside of our inner experience of it, all that matters for our study is that when we look inside at consciousness, at mind and inner-subjective self, *there is blue experience*, and that blue experience is in the mind, not in the world (it is not where the sky is, your experience of the sky is not up in the sky, it is where you are, where your mind is, which most people believe is in the brain, and the blueness experience is not in the brain: there is no blue thing in the brain, such as a blue visual screen, or you would have a medical emergency!). Therefore, the blue-experience is not in physical reality—it is part of nonphysical mind content.

The professional academics are not unaware of the rock-solid argumentation (proofs) for the nonphysicality of consciousness, developed by professional philosophers, and which have existed for decades, as is well-known in professional academia. I say this because the blue sky experience I just referred to follows from the following argument, developed in and known about for a long time in professional philosophy, as presented here by the *Stanford Encyclopedia of Philosophy*:

   1. Bertie is experiencing a green thing.

2. Suppose that there is no physical green thing outside Bertie's head.[10]

But

3. There is no physical green thing inside Bertie's head either.
4. If it is physical, the green thing is either outside Bertie's head or inside it. Thus,
5. The green thing is not physical. [1,2,3,4] Thus,
6. Berties' experience contains a nonphysical thing. [1,5] Thus,
7. Bertie's experience is not, or not entirely, physical. [6] (Lycan 2015, 5)

The article's author for this *Stanford Encyclopedia of Philosophy* entry comments after the argument, saying: "This is a valid deductive argument against materialism, and its premises are hard to deny" (Ibid.).

An argument with an inference this strong would *normally*, for any other subject-matter, be considered to give a conclusion that could be trusted. But professional academics go against the simple reasoning and cannot accept this, because if they accept it, then the man-is-a-spirit argument for the existence of God immediately follows. The typical academic will not accept the ironclad logic of this argument, and will instead imply or assert that there must be an error somewhere, as we saw Law try to do above. The professional academic will instead claim that brain-meat produces the *illusion* of an inner spirit (which leads to the contradiction that external physical matter could produce/create an inner spirit—which is like saying pure dryness produces the thorough wetness). The professional academic,

---

[10] What this is referring to is the idea that reality is, in fact, colorless: since atoms are colorless and external reality is therein colorless, wherein color experience of the world must be a product of the mind *self-creating* color-experience when observing matter objects, which are, ultimately, colorless atomic patterns. We will see in Chapter 7 that reality *must* contain partless atoms (philosophical atoms), and cannot be atomless (or what professional philosophers sometimes call 'atomless gunk').

will side-step this *Stanford Encyclopedia* argument, and despite having no other real argumentation for what the inner spirit-self is, will argue for the opposite of the conclusion of this argument: that directly observable mind/consciousness, which has seemingly zero physical properties, and looks entirely like something that is an ingredient of a spirit, is somehow, nevertheless, to be considered as *physical* and *nonspiritual*, despite there being no evidence whatsoever. This is like saying a red marble is a blue marble.

It is almost as if we go through our lives, moment-to-moment, always looking outwardly at physical objects, very rarely, if ever, looking inwardly at inner mind contents, where when we finally do close our eyes, for example, pause, and take a good look inside of our selves, it will either be for a fleeting second, hardly noticing what is inside of mind and consciousness, *or* a person will be so accustomed to physical objects with physical properties that they will not recognize the differentness of a nonphysical item with nonphysical properties. And there is seemingly a consequent tendency, perhaps, to want to claim that the inwardly viewed mind as nonphysical is actually an illusion, and it is actually physical, since one's mind is so accustomed to outer-physical objects. But that would be to make a fallacious move, as illustrated in this example, where the blue marbles represent all the physical objects one experiences from moment-to-moment, and the one red marble is the observation of inner consciousness:

> Consider a gigantic tub of ten billion blue marbles, and a single red one. And imagine that you live in it, for your entire life, and so far all you've seen while "swimming around" in the marbles are the blue ones, wherein all that you know (all that you are familiar with) are the blue

marbles. But imagine that one day, as you are "swimming" through your marble world, you come across the single red marble in the giant tub, and since you've seen only blue ones so far, you conclude (using the above formula we used from Stephen Law's "reasoning"):

> I can directly see that the one marble is red, in contrast to the ten billon, but I should believe that it is not blue, what I am seeing is an illusion, and it is blue. (This is Law's formula.)

The one red marble represents the inner mind observed as nonphysical, such as the first time a person turns their gaze inward and sees they have a consciousness,[11] and it looks nothing like the rest of the reality they've seen. But asserting that mind is physical, is a worse situation than the marbles conclusion, since in the case of the marbles, only *one* property was flipped—the marble was red not blue (but was still spherical, presumably the same size, etc.)—but in the case of mind being compared to the items of the world, seemingly all properties of a subjective item of consciousness (such as a feeling) are the inverse of an external matter object.

If the professional academic admits what is directly viewable—that the mind inside looks like a spirit—then the professional academic would have to transform into a theologian. It is not within the professional academics' job description to admit that direct observation of self reveals that the inner self has a lack of material-physical properties, and is composed of nonphysical, spiritual-like ingredients. The professional academic is paid to study the *physical* world, not that which is nonphysical and therefore spiritual, and if he

---

[11] When I was still teaching in the universities, I recall when the subject-matter about consciousness would come up during introductory classes, I often would have students say (surprising) things to me like, "I really like this part of the class, it makes me really think about what I am—I never really knew that I had feelings, or that my feelings were an entity." It was as if they did not even know the constituents of their mind and self fully existed.

begins to talk about the spirituality of inner-mind and self, he will immediately come-across as a theologian or a monk, where it will seem that the best book for him to research will be the Bible, rather than Bertrand Russell.

And even more disquieting for the professional academic, is that if self clearly looks like a spirit, then the professional academic has to immediately shutter at the next possible move, which is the idea that the "spirit" referred to in the man-is-a-spirit argument is the Christian God, and that the nature of self is entirely in agreement with the Bible:

> _God_ is the Spirit that created human spirit-minds.

These are reasons why the professional academic tells us that when you see your inner mind and self as a nonphysical entity, you in fact cannot be witnessing what you think are viewing.

The professional academic wants us to trust _him or her_ on this (nonevidential) point, but the direct experience (direct _evidence_) of my nonphysical inner self is _convincing_; and seeing it within, is a somewhat startling observation:

> The inner consciousness is unlike anything else one can see in their daily life, where all that one can see in daily life has physical properties (location, extension, colorfulness, spatial motion, temporality, and so forth), except one thing: _you_ (the mind, consciousness, self, within).

Self/mind is unlike anything in the cause-and-effect natural world, and for that reason we would apparently be nonlogical to conclude that self/mind has a source (a cause) that comes from anything in the natural world (the natural cannot originate/cause the non-natural, the transcendent). There is nothing complicated about this; it is just that our minds are not used to the *mysterium tremendum* of the pure and simple logic revealed in actual reality.

> If we merely accept where simple-but-beautiful logic leads, where observation and reason actually take us, rather than relying on our own minds and (incomplete) ideas, we will find unfathomable significance to our lives—but only to our lives *in the Spirit (God-Christ) that created us*, not in the ways of the world, which do not satisfy, which lead to trouble (John 16:33).

A spirit must originate from the spiritual, and as just stated, the non-spiritual cannot cause/create the spiritual—just as what is fully dry cannot in itself make wetness (non-water cannot turn into water). It does not appear that a spirit can be created, having spirit-properties, being caused by that which has no spirit-properties—for if the nonspiritual could create the spiritual, where would spiritual constituents come-into-existence from, if they cannot come from that which is devoid of spiritual constituents?

Professional academics write book-after-book, containing all sorts of complicated and sometimes even hard-to-believe theses for how the mystery and nonphysicality of consciousness is the product of a hunk of meat in one's head. Yet I can merely look inside myself, introspecting, directly observing my consciousness *to directly see what it is*—so why do I need only my brain to discover what my consciousness is? Why would I study *only* the wood if I want to know what the *fire* in my fireplace is? A feeling in me looks like an ingredient of a spirit-being, so why do I need to analyze what that spirit-being-ingredient is like by only considering the aspects of the meat-computer it allegedly interacts with and/or is allegedly identical to (according to the professional academic)? When I study the fire, I don't feel any sort of urgency to demand that the fire _is identical to_ the wood, since they obviously appear to be completely different items, with completely different and in many ways opposite properties, nevertheless operating in a continuous system. In a roughly analogous way, the meat-computer and the inwardly observed spirit surely don't look anything like each other. I can know that each exists (but note that knowing inner consciousness is a far more direct, immediate knowing than knowing the existence of brain-matter, which is witnessing neuronal brain activity patterns indirectly via the brain-scanner screen), but one (mind) is identified, felt, to be _the self_, where the other (brain-meat) is not. If a person has their brain but not their mind removed (such as if mind could be downloaded onto a supercomputer), one will still feel themselves _to be the same self_, but if a mind is removed and the brain remains, the person will _not_ feel as if they still have, or are, a self. What we feel, observe, verify, and discover when we go and search for what the mind-self is, is not meat, but is a spirit: a collection of feelings, thoughts, and inner picture images, qualia, which the professional academic asks us to believe is produced by complicated meat. But which argument makes more sense:

1. When I look at my self inwardly, I see a nonphysical mind.
2. Therefore, my inner self is created by a nonphysical thing (a Spirit).

Or,

1. When I look at my self inwardly, I see a nonphysical mind.
2. Therefore, I am created by complicated physical meat.

From thorough dryness comes wetness.

Logic only supports the top argument, and the bottom argument is a contradiction, much like the following "argument" (non-argument) is a contradiction:

1. I see an entity E that has properties a, b, c, and d.
2. Therefore, E subsists and is created by something with no commonalities to E, and which has properties not-a, not-b, not-c, and not-d.

A feeling, for example, does not have a colorful surface, a known location in space, and it does not seem to have solidity or extension—*it does not have any of these physical properties*. But how, then, can I call it physical at all? Wouldn't I call something physical if it, in fact, *has* physical properties in the first place?

Does Brain Damage Prove the Mind is Only a Brain State?

Often it is claimed that mind is nothing more than brain or brain state, since often there are precise correlations between mind activity and brain damage that occur (such as one specific area of brain being damage repeatedly leading to similar language problems in a person). The professional academic tells us that since mind and brain have repeatable *correlations* of activity, such as brain cells activating in correlation with mind experience (a predictable part of the brain becomes active when measured under the brain-scanner when specific thought and feeling activities are taking place), this serves as evidence that inner-subjective mind/consciousness is describable as being no more than physical brain activity. But how do these ideas lead to the conclusion that mind can be described in terms of only the brain? Why do we collapse mind down to brain, and not, instead, collapse brain up to mind[12]? But more importantly,

> *If mind and brain were systems that are in sync, as would be expected if a human mind uses a human brain and CNS to manage a human body, shouldn't we expect mind and brain to be in predictable—even very tightly predictable—synchronization? Wouldn't we even expect nonphysical mind to operate in <u>specific</u> parts of the brain-meat machinery?[13]*

The idea that brain and mind correlating indicates that one is identical to the other (that mind is reducible to brain/brain-state), is a correlation vs. causation critical thinking fallacy: the fallacy of seeing two events correlate in time, and believing there is causation involved, rather than mere correlation, and where causation has not been verified. How is causation known to exist in any given situation? The answer is that if A causes B, if we remove A, then B will not occur.[14] One can add and subtract A at will, and each time B relates perfectly: remove A, and B vanishes, add A, and B again will appear. This can be done repeatedly, that is causation, and it is the heart of science (the pure idea of what science is). Anything else will be only verifiable as being correlation, at best—which is the case with mind patterns

---

[12] This is the move is the move that, for example, the philosophical idealist would make.

[13] I believe these arguments do succeed in avoiding the claim that brain damage victims verify that mind is just an aspect of brain, but beyond that, I actually don't hold too much importance to these claims, since they lean toward mind-body dualism. I don't find as much harm in mind-body dualism as others do, but the bigger point is that I am a simulation theorist (nonphysical Calvinist), and simulation theory avoids mind-body dualism, makes it an irrelevant topic.

[14] For those interested in occasionalist causation, that would not be a relevant topic here. I am only discussing so-called *scientific* causation here, which would be "downstream" of any discussion of occasionalist causation.

and neural brain firing patterns, those are correlation, not established as causation, as I will go into further now.

There are very specific scientific cases that show that *mind is present without brain*, or without brain functioning in any expected way, which would extinguish the idea that mind reduces to brain, and which would show that idea to be the aforementioned causation vs. correlation critical thinking fallacy. We will study those below, and again in Chapter 9—and the evidence is clear and definitive—a game-changer—coming from the journals and discoveries of professional science. The evidence presented in Chapter 9 comes from the study of hydrocephalics. (If the reader would like to peruse that extremely important information now, before continuing with this chapter, that information can be found in Chapter 9 in the discussion about Jack Gallant's research about the primary visual cortex (PVC), or go to the Index and look up "hydrocephalics" for the page number in Chapter 10.) I realize that many will disregard this information as too difficult to believe, but what is being said here about these issues, and what is shown about them in this book, does definitively disprove the idea that mind is caused solely by brain and CNS—and if it is not, then mind *is a spirit*. So, as I was indicating, mind being equal to brain-state is straightforwardly shown to be a correlation-as-causation critical thinking fallacy. Academics are eager to point out how brain damage correlates with mind-activity reduction in predictable ways, but they are thoroughly reluctant to discuss when the opposite verifiably happens: when stunning brain damage and/or brain reduction leads to either zero effect, *or* leads to increased consciousness[15].

---

[15] As mentioned, the specific, and rather shocking, example of this is studied in Chapter 10 below. But furthermore, there are many widely-known professional studies that show that brain damage is not

Mysterium Tremendum

As mentioned in the previous section, premise 1 of the man-is-a-spirit argument—that mind is verifiably nonphysical—is the correct position, as this entire chapter discusses—or, in other words, I do not know how to avoid that conclusion, given all that is said in this chapter. The more one delves into that finding, the more it is verified. And that conclusion ultimately proves that God—and the Christian God, as this book will show—is real, and is the Creator of all things.

If the reader has a case of cognitive dissonance over these issues, or is just having difficulty undoing the conditioning that their minds have received since youth in being taught the nonscientific[16], non-verifiable thesis that mind is physical, I suggest that the reader deeply ponder (i) the evidence of this chapter, and (ii) the fact that _evidence_, not assumption, is what establishes knowledge, and what establishes what is real vs. what is imagination. If one contemplatively, determinably embarks on (i) and (ii) deeply, perhaps even making it a saturating meditation project encompassing their life for a few days, that should largely dislodge, and/or undo the conditioning of the error of the mind-is-physical fallacy that has been conditioned, and one will start to absorb the verifiable truth, the logic of reality, as is shown in the man-is-

---

uncommonly linked to increase in spiritual experience and mystical experience, wherein it may be theorized that such increase of mystical consciousness could result in increase of certain types of intelligences.

[16] I don't say this to be derogatory toward the academic view that mind is physical, but rather, I only say that the academic view is _nonscientific_ for the simple and uncontroversial fact that mind-is-physical concept is thoroughly a _philosophical topic_, not a scientific finding that we can all go and verify today if we wanted to. This is not secret, and the academic will, I believe, in general freely admit this and have no angst. Many professional academics will, however, resort to the brain damage findings of the previous section as possible or even likely verification of their mind-is-solely-physical theory, but as we saw in that section, and as will be further confirmed in Chapter 10, that is in fact a critical thinking fallacy, not a scientific finding.

a-spirit argument, and as the rest of this book shows, that the "spirit" in the conclusion of the argument is Christ. *Mysterium tremendum*.

So why does the contemporary academic conduct matters in this nonacademic, non-inferential manner, when it comes to consciousness? My purported answer is that the supernaturality of consciousness is too powerful, mysterious, surreal, unknown, or mystical to simply *accept or look-at* (observe, analyze) for the professional academic. It is too euphoric, too powerful (in its otherness, in its sense of being *different* than what one is accustomed to), and often even too dark for academics to directly study and delve into, where in probing directly into mind could feel like venturing into what could possibly lead to severe cognitive dissonance, causing one to transform into a poet or artist. So, it is not possible that professional academics opt to study the inner world (mind, self, consciousness) by looking at it—for if they looked at it, they could be moved into its supernaturality. Go and sit in a dark closet for just five or ten minutes, and *focus*: meditate deeply on how everything you witness in your inner self/mind cannot be found to have any physical qualities, simply come to terms with that observable fact, and you will brush up against the *mysterium tremendum* of actual reality (and you could be turned into a poet or theologian).

The Overdetermination "Problem"

Often the professional academic, in attempting to explain how mental effects have physical causes, will claim that including conscious subjectivity is not required for explaining behavior. In exploring how a physical event (such as pushing a button) can be traced back to a brain event (working backwards:

(3) finger pushes the button, (2) nerve signals sent from brain to hand, (1) brain state associated with mental event of *wanting* to push the button), we arrive at the professional academic's widely discussed *overdetermination problem*. This problem involves the idea that brain activity already accounts for the (1) cause, that leads to (2) and (3), so asserting that an inner mental/subjective event is *also* needed would be causal overdetermination (the cause is believed, by the professional academic, to be already accounted for in brain activity, so adding *more* causation by suggesting that the inner subjective event is needed is overdetermined causation).

However, this line of reasoning involving the overdetermination problem has obvious problems. The above (1)➔(2)➔(3) argument assumes that (1) can happen without needing to refer to (0) nonphysical subjective experience (where, of course, (0) would not be detected via the brain-scanner, thus leading to the obvious *illusion* that only (1) existed, rather than (0)➔(1)), as impetus for the pushing the button. The academic, here, is merely trying to say that meat (brain) pushed the button, (1)➔(2)➔(3), and it is not the case that the (0) inwardly verifiably existing inner-subjective feeling pushed the button, (0)➔(1)➔(2)➔(3). The overdetermination problem simply assumes that the brain activity is the first step. How do we *know* a purely nonphysical mental event did not precede the initial brain measurement? Answer: *because we can see it in our consciousness!* If the professional academic admits (0), that would lead to the conclusion that (0) and therefore (1) was created by God.

The academic will want to urge that (1) is, in fact, identical to (0), and that all subjectivity believed to exist can be explained as properties of the brain-firing stage (1). But this is to give-rise to the same problem referred to above: how can (1) brain-meat activity be equal to (0) nonphysically appearing subjective experience, when (1) and (0) have *opposite* qualities: brain-meat activity (neural firing activity) certainly does not look like the inwardly verifiable subjective experience of having a *feeling* of wanting to push the button. When I am looking at a piece of meat, it does not seem like I am looking at a feeling, and when I am looking directly at an inner feeling, it sure does not have any meat-like properties. Indeed, those two—meat and feeling—have opposite properties of each other—so are we not forced to abandon the professional philosopher's claim that (0) = (1), that the meat is the inner subjective experience? How can it be that the professional academic feels comfortable suggesting that when I look inside at my subjective mind, which appears devoid of physical properties, in any way tell me I am looking at a hunk of meat? That I am looking at anything physical at all?

I believe it is safe to say that with the overdetermination problem, the professional academic is trying to merely side-step (0) subjectivity from the discussion, to make it an epiphenomenalist inconsequential side-effect, in order to claim that all mind activity = brain activity, as I just explained. But again, until one can show how my inner feeling that I can clearly "see" inside of myself is identical to, and has the same properties as, a hunk of meat (some chunk of my brain), logic *forces* me to hold that (1) =/= (0), that (0) is upstream of (1), *wherein without (0), (1) would not happen*: take away (0) and (1) will not occur.

But Who Is the "Spirit" that Created Me?

In my life, I have learned to trust basic logic and evidence, and when I do, I have at times seen *great* discoveries follow. The man-is-a-spirit argument, the topic of this chapter, is just such a discovery. It may be hard to grasp, mind-blowing, difficult for you to fully absorb, to fully accept the pure and simple logic of the argument, since you have likely been conditioned, probably since you were very young, to believe the philosophy of physicalism (that which exists, or which can be experienced, are *only* physical items), and often with such conditioning it is hard to *unbelieve*, no matter how stringent the counter-evidence. In that case, and as was said above, the cure is to contemplate, explore, dwell-on, be obsessed with this topic—with the man-is-a-spirit argument, because after you explore it long enough, become accustomed to it enough, you will start to overcome mental conditioning and accept where the logic, the evidence takes us—logic and evidence always win-out over nonevidential belief, to understate the issue.

Here again is the argument that I call *the man-is-a-spirit argument for the existence of God*:

1. When doing introspection, I can see that my thoughts, my feelings, my mind, are viewed to be *nonphysical*, and resemble a spirit, not a matter-brain or brain-state.
2. Only a spirit can cause/create a spirit to exist.
3. <u>Conclusion</u>: I am created by a spirit, rather than by a natural process from external reality.

In a few paragraphs I will present reasoning that appears to strongly verify that the "spirit" referred to in the conclusion is the Christian God, and if that is so, the existence of the Christian God is confirmed by thoroughly verifiable findings, via the inner verification of what mind-self is (nonphysical spirit).

Notice that the verifiability of the man-is-a-spirit argument has the opposite approach, the opposite level of confirmation, as compared to the academics' claims about mind:

- The academic theory of mind (that it is a brain state) is *thoroughly* theoretical and without any verifiable evidence (as discussed above), and
- The Christian theory of mind—that man is a spirit—is thoroughly verifiable, in the most direct possible way, confirmed by the strongest possible evidence (evidence that bypasses the limitations and problems of sensation-based information).

These are truly significant details. What I am calling the Christian theory of mind is genuinely based in better conformational grounds than any scientific position can be—and add to that, that the professional academic view of mind is not even at the level of being scientific (it is a pre-scientific theory). The man-is-a-spirit argument is *also* not a scientific argument, since it is *not* based in verification and analysis via sensation (which is a requirement of science), but that would however seem not a fault of the man-is-a-spirit argument, and it is clearly a benefit, for the same reasons that Descartes found "I think therefore I am to be more reliable than any other information. The man-is-a-spirit argument is a higher level of verification.[17]

---

[17] I am actually understating this issue, in my opinion. The professional philosopher and academic discusses how the problems with the reliability of information about the external world are: (1) empirical information is dependent on imperfect sensation, and (2) experience of *outer*-world items happens in the *inner* mind, not where the experience external/outside-world item being perceived is located at (in simpler terms, when I see an apple, what I see is a picture in my mind, and I am not experiencing the apple where

Regardless of what my brain-meat is like, or of how advanced of a supercomputer I imagine it to be, it is not something that I can see, can observe. But my mental content, my moment-to-moment mind itself, my experiencing, is directly observable. But my inwardly observable, and directly observable mind *is not experienceable or describable in physical terms*, and it is therefore nonphysical—resembling a spirit—and that leads to the conclusion that the origin of my mind is spiritual (mind is created by a spirit). How could the logic be simpler than this? If one simply looks at mind to find out what mind is, directly analyzing it's nonphysicality, the apparent supernaturality (beyond nature, beyond naturalism) of mind becomes the immediate, and primary study of the analysis of the mind—since that is what one finds when studying mind on *its* terms.

Some may also object to the idea that a creator God is the "spirit" I am referring to in this chapter. In other words, somebody could pose the following objection to what I have written:

> I agree that we are spirits created by some other spirit. But my problem is this: I see no reason why the spirit has to be any sort of creator-God, or the Christian God. Why can't it just be another very powerful supernatural entity, perhaps even powerful beyond our imagination, but why would it need to be within the definition of being a "creator-God"?

By definition, a spirit is nonphysical, and so, any two spirits will have at least that resemblance to each other, in that they are both *nonphysical*, and they are both *spirits*. In addition, I know that I am a self, a "me", an "I", an "I am".

---

it is, sitting on the table at a distance from my head). Verification of the nature of inner mind (as nonphysical) does not involve either of these problems, and therein is a more reliable form of verification.

I can even "see", or detect, this *I am* within, with direct introspective reflection, where I have awareness of I am/self: I can feel, apprehend my self (I am). I can see and feel myself within *having awareness*, and by that I have knowledge that I am a self, a "me", an experiencing mind: an *I am*. "I am" is a description of self, of me, the holder of mind, the center of inner consciousness. In being a description of me, it is like a name, in that it only refers to me. Your *I am* denotes your innermost haecceity[18], and mine denotes mine. My *I am* is my name, and yours is yours. We each have the same name, and thus we have some tremendous resemblance to each other, as if we humans all have a likeness, a oneness (see Phil. 2:2, Rom. 12:5, John 17:21), all of the *Imago Dei*. That we all refer to ourselves by the name "I am" has an apparently hitherto unseen issue: it tells us who the "spirit" is in the man-is-a-spirit argument.

We Have the Same Name (I am) as God (I AM that I AM)

It would appear safe to conclude that the nonphysical Spirit that created me *also* has a self, since it seems that, by definition, any nonphysical spirit will be, or have, a self: it will be a thinking and experiencing entity that has awareness and has a haecceity, with some sort of capacity to act in ways that mind-containing items act. If the spirit that created me is also a self, then it also is describable as an *I am*—we have the same name. The purest description, for who and what *I am*, is that my nonphysical self is described

---

[18] Here is the dictionary definition of haecceity:
    Definition of haecceity
    : the status of being an individual or a particular nature : INDIVIDUALITY, SPECIFICITY, THISNESS
    specifically : what makes something to be an ultimate reality different from any other.
From: https://www.merriam-webster.com/dictionary/haecceity.

as an "I am." So, there is a resemblance between me, you, all people, and the spirit that created me: we are all nonphysical spirits that are described by the name, _I am_. In different words, by using the simple and reliable verification that _I am_ is a nonphysical item as a starting point, simple logic will show us that my name is _I am_, your name is _I am_, the spirit which created us is named _I am_:

> We (you, me, and the spirit that created us) all have the same name, and even though we all can be verified to have non-identical haecceities (I can look within and see that I am only _my_ haecceity, not yours, for example), by having the same name we have some not-fully-understood but nevertheless _tremendous resemblance_ to each other.

We only need to directly work from, and within, the bounds of the man-is-a-spirit argument to get to that these findings. You probably have not thought of it, but all people are using the same name to refer to each other: _I am_.

So, we should expect that there is another spirit that exists that is the other _I am_, who has identified itself as being the one that created us, that created my mind-self, and your mind-self, and who is the very spirit denoted in the conclusion of the man-is-a-spirit argument. I say this because, as introduced in the previous paragraph, we resemble the nonphysical _I am_ that created us, so if it wants us to know who it is (and Chapter 3 will show us He _does_ want us to know, in specific ways), the Creator-I-AM will tell us, and it would make sense to do so by name: _I am_. This Creator-I-am would be the only other "entity" described by the name _I am_ in all of existence, if that Creator wanted us to be able to clearly to be pointed-out, known, identified by those who see beyond their own I am, and see the logic of reality, which reveals the Creator-I-am.

I AM that I AM (YHVH)

There is only one instance of a creator-Spirit I know of referred to by the name of *I am*—which is, in fact, the only other entity I know of in all of existence, that is named and/or described by "I am"—and that is the Christian God of the Bible (YHVH), He is "the Great I AM," or "I AM that I AM" (Ex. 3:14).

So, it would appear that our human essence, our identifies and haecceities, as nonphysical spirits, contain a signature in them, where the only *other* thing in all of our known reality that has been presented to us that has the *I am* in its name-description, in its signature, *is the Christian God* (YHVH). The same term, "I am", only denotes two things in all of known reality: human selves, and the creator-God of the Bible. God has been hidden in plain sight, and He has been telling us, by name, who He is, and that we are His creations. The "spirit" in the man-is-a-spirit argument is the Christian God.

It is by the very purest and simplest viewable information that exists, and the purest and simplest of logical principles, that has brought us to this discovery. In the elementary structure and makeup of reality is written the proof of the existence of God (YHVH). His *signature* is built into the totality and essence of *your* being and self. This discovery has always been closer to you than anything, all you ever had to do was look at the directly viewable reality of your nonphysical self, to discover it is different from, and could not be created by, the external, physical reality, and that it could only be created by a Creator (I AM that I AM).

Work Cited

Lycan, William, "Representational Theories of Consciousness", _The Stanford Encyclopedia of Philosophy_ (Summer 2015 Edition), Edward N. Zalta (ed.), URL = <https://plato.stanford.edu/archives/sum2015/entries/consciousness-representational/>.

2. The Solution to the Problem of Evil

Part 1: Introduction

The fact that the things that God creates are things that are *distinct* from Himself, is an often overlooked issue in theology, but in fact it leads to and involves answers to the biggest theological cruxes, such as why is there pain, or why is God defined as pure love when His Creation has sinful creatures in it. In Chapter 1 we discovered a direct proof for the existence of God (YHVH), based on pure logic, and the simplest and most reliable information there is ("I think therefore I am"). In this chapter, we will build on our discoveries, and find out why the creation of God (our physical reality) involves so much pain and so many defects, or deviations from His ways (such deviations are *sin*). I do not believe the discoveries of this chapter have been unveiled previously. Finding out why will also reveal precisely *why* God does not *stop* the pain, sin and evil, which will furthermore directly lead to the logical finding (and spiritual revelation) that our reality, in order that it continue to exist, involve an ontology of redemption by the Creator. Like the discoveries of Chapter 1, our findings in this chapter will be found to be built into the basic logic of the fabric of reality. The logical discoveries enclosed in this chapter are direct, mathematical in precision and tightness, and like the findings of other chapters in this book, seem to reveal that the logic and truth of God, permeating every aspect of our existence, constitutes a hitherto unseen logic of ultimate reality.

Two of the most serious unsolved problems that remain in Christian theology are (1) why is there pain? and (2) why is there sin? In other words, why is this world so dreadful, with so many hurting people, rampant poverty, illness, and misery, and how could there be sin—*all in a universe created by an all-loving God?* These are truly critical questions, and their being unanswered, I think it's safe to say, keeps huge numbers of people from turning to the God of the Bible. In this chapter, I will present what I am very confident is an entirely simple, logically certain, and undeniable argument that explains that this sort of reality, that involves pain and sin, *is the only sort of reality that God can create.* Let me put that in more precise wording:

> Absolutely anything and everything that the creator-God creates, while initially can only be all-good, since a perfect God can *only* create that which is *good*, but the creations of God can nevertheless *only be imperfect*, as will explained below, despite being all-good, and therefore likely self-generate pain and sin, for seemingly most universes and realities created by God.[19]

Again, these problems have been hitherto unsolved in Christian theology. Consider what RC Sproul, one of the most famous Calvinist/Reformed theologians of the past 50 years, says about this issue:

> Before I go any further to answer the question of where evil came from, I have to give my short answer to the question, my down-and-dirty answer to the question, *Where did evil come from?* And my answer is this: *I don't know.* So maybe it's time for me to just sit down...
>
> I don't know how to explain the origin of evil, and what else I can tell you is that I am sure that in this world I will never be able to answer

---

[19] In Grupp 2018b, in addition to several writings in the works, and in an argument below in this chapter, I find that the best interpretation for the Christian creator-Trinity/God is that He is a perpetual creator of infinite creativity, creating *infinite* worlds and realities. An argument in Chapter 4 also comes to this same conclusion.

that question. I don't know of any philosopher or theologian who has answered it adequately, at least to satisfy my mind, and I am sure that I'm not going to go beyond the insights of Augustine, Aquinas, Calvin, Luther, Edwards and the rest, who had wrestled with this…

What is evil… is the easy part of the two questions, the second part,… How evil could intrude into a universe created by a God who is all-together holy, all-together righteous, and not only is this universe created by such a God, but it is also *governed* and *ruled* by such a God, and *if* this God is holy, and *if* this God is righteous, how in-the-world can He tolerate so much evil in it. The origin of evil has been called the Achilles heel of Christianity… the supreme point of vulnerability. If God is all-powerful, and has the power to create a universe without evil, or has the power to rid the universe of evil and… He doesn't do it then He's not good.[20]

So the specific question we are interested in, is:

If there is a perfect Creator, made of perfect love, who is infinite and can do anything (nothing is impossible with God) why couldn't He simply have the capacity to create humans as free beings, who genuinely love Him, and who can exist in absolute joy of God without all the pain and suffering and misery of this universe, and without the Fall in Genesis 3?

I want to be specific that, in this chapter, I will *not* claim that the problem of evil is solved by referring to human free-will as being the culprit, and I will not explore the topic of how sin (and consequent pain) derive from human free-

---

[20] Idea Pump, Oct. 27, 2013, "What Is Evil & Where Did It Come From? - RC Sproul", YouTube.com, https://www.youtube.com/watch?v=5Ir6pKEV0RQ.

will. The widely claimed view that human free-will _is_ the reason the Fall of Creation happened is, strictly speaking, _correct_, for our specific universe, and it is the reason we have sin and pain in our reality. However, the problem is that using this "explanation" does not solve the problem of evil, and it merely leaves us with the problem of evil in the form of this question: _How did human choice generate a sin?_ And consequently, we are still left with the problem: Where did pain and sin come from? How did our reality created by an infinitely loving, good, and intelligent creator-God obtain them?

For these reasons, using free-will as an explanation for the problem of evil fails, and thus is problematical and often futile in ministry and in theological work. If humans understood the mystery of free-will better, perhaps it could be understood how human choice can lead to the nothingness of sin, but free-will, human free-choice, is a thorough mystery. The problem of evil plagues us by therein leaving the existence of sin and pain unexplained. For these reasons, we need an explanation that does not involve or even elude to human choice or free-will.

But the mysteries of the problem of evil and sin are actually even quite a bit worse than this, for even if we had full understanding of the detailed and specific mechanics of free-will choice in human consciousnesses, it still would simply not help in answer this question:

> _Why won't God_ <u>_stop_</u> _the misery, the pain, the bloodshed, the poverty, the horror everywhere!_

Pretend we do have full understanding of human free-will, and do we see perfectly how it leads to sin and pain in Genesis 3:6—alas, it likely does us no good, because it leaves wide-open the following truly serious questions for Christian theology:

- Why couldn't God create reality in a way where our free-will did not lead to such pervasive and gut-wrenching sin, pain, and suffering world-wide?

- Can't we humans be free without the horror of the pain of reality?

- Free-will is utterly mysterious, seemingly a creation ex nihilo—how does it work? Especially in a universe with seemingly so much determinism?[21]

- If God is infinitely wise and powerful, couldn't He have created a reality that accomplished what He wanted without being such a horrific and painful reality, pervaded by so much evil and sin, and which contains creatures that genuinely love Him with true free-willed love?

Even a full understanding of free will, and how it solves the problem of evil, may not be able to answer these questions. I have heard Christians throughout my life try to side-step these questions, saying, "oh, we just can't understand God's ways." That is true, *but* that is not a good answer, and these are, in fact, *really good questions*, where people inevitably are going to be irked by them (including some life-long Christians, such as those who have undergone serious tragedy, and wonder how God can allow the misery). So, the point is,

> *Even if we understood how free will was legitimately a cause of the problem of evil, it really does us no good, and we still have no explanation for why God created, sustains, and allows a reality that contains sin and pain.*

---

[21] I discussed free will as being supernatural and *ex nihilo* creation, in Grupp 2018a. I will have more development of the concepts from Grupp 2018a in an upcoming article.

So, here is an understatement: A new argument is needed to show why reality, created by a perfect and good God of infinite love, has sin, evil and pain. We need an argument that really gets the job done, to end this question, this issue, by showing that this is how reality _has to be_, how God _could only_ create it, and how the logic of our reality clearly shows this is just how things had to be—_anything else is clearly logically impossible_. It can't be an argument that ultimately just dodges the issue (as all other "solutions" to the problem of evil seem to do), but on that really shows, plain-as-day, that the logic of existence is such that if anything exists, if any reality is created by God, it will be corrupted and need to be redeemed. In simpler terms: _we need a reason—I mean we really need a good reason!—for why an infinitely good God created this horror-show reality!_[22]

That is what I will reveal in this chapter, which is a discovery about our physical reality that is desperately needed by the people of this lost world that is fading away (1 John 2:17). Specifically, the findings of this chapter uncover the following:

> Specifically _why_ our existence in this physical reality has pain and sin is built into the structure and mechanics of our reality, of our existence—and into _anything_ created by an absolutely perfect monotheistic creator-God—where by the logic of the Creator-created relationship, the only way anything can exist, can be created, is to

---

[22] Some readers may think I am overdoing it here, and reality is not so bad that it can be described as a _horror-show_. I would like to refer those readers to the book of 2 Kings (among several others in the OT), which show the truly dire nature of this physical reality. And I would like to invite those readers to come to the jail I work at, to do ministry through the bars, to experience the daily misery, tears, mental illness, demon possession, physical illness, violence, hatred, and so forth. I would like to invite those readers to read the pages of history, to travel to the slums of Asia, to do ministry in the inner city, and so forth. If you do not agree with my points, I would guess you are blocking out the real nature of reality with television, money obsession, denial, and addictions.

develop in such a way where they are *just* like things are now: filled and/or affected by sin and pain.

The Creator cannot create the sin and pain, but as we will see in a moment, the only way any reality can exist is if the Creator-God creates a reality that will inevitably *fall into* what humans now live in, in this fallen, pain-filled, evil-influenced physical reality.

Part 2: The Argument

The argument below shows that for the Creator-God create anything, the only thing He will create is that which collapses into sin and pain, would not follow logic, and thus any pre-redeemed reality will only be roughly like what ours like, as far as pain and sin are concerned.

To my knowledge, this argument has, surprisingly, not been presented before this time, despite its simplicity and rudimentary nature, and even though it does lurk deep in some of the theological concepts found in the Bible. This argument can be a *tremendous*, even *miraculous* asset in ministry, which has been the sole objective in developing the argument, since the argument will quickly, definitively, and authoritatively addresses the following reasonable and justified question so often asked by atheists, non-believers, skeptics of Christianity, and people genuinely just curious (including Christians) as to why

> *Of all the things a loving and perfectly good God could do, why would He create <u>this</u> particular physical reality we humans live in, that now contains pain, suffering, confusion, darkness, evil, and sin? Why would the infinite God of love create a reality like that?*

In my experience in ministry, nothing turns away believers more than this particular legitimate question. People are genuinely confused, and the question is a more-than-reasonable one.

I will first spell-out the argument and the answer in detail, and then present the 10 second version that can be used quickly, on-the-spot, during storm of situations of gritty ministry.

Argument Stipulation: An *absolutely* perfect monotheistic creator-I AM that I AM (God/YHVH) exists, as proven in Chapter 1, where He is the only absolute perfection, nothing can be added to Him to improve-upon the perfect creator God, no higher being can be conceived. There is only one Perfect, and therefore it should be capitalized. And everything that is not the one Perfect is distinct from Him, and is not describable as being perfect.

The Argument:

1. If God creates anything at all, what He creates will be *distinct* from Himself, *different* from Himself, so that what is created will not be identical to God, as is necessary if God creates anything whatsoever.

2. What God creates, in being *distinct* from Himself, will therein *not* be absolutely perfect, and can only be lower-than God (it will be *good*, but not absolutely perfect).

3. That which is lower-than God, and *different* from God, is *not-God* (and not Godly), and that which is not-God is imperfect, incomplete, deviating from perfection.

4. (From 3) A reality with not-Godly (unGodly) elements will *inevitably* develop regions where there are concentrations and higher densities of what is unGodly, since

(i)   elements of unGodliness in the creation will inevitably interact, and by interacting will multiply their levels of unGodliness (I call this *the gravitation model of sin*, and I will break it down in the paragraphs below), and since

(ii) all of the created reality *can only be* imperfect-unGodly, and thus any bunching-up of unGodly reality leads to foci, or even density imploding zones (singularity), of unGodliness.

5. God cannot create sinfulness, so the reality created by God, being different form God, will be inevitably be prone to internally-generated, self-caused unGodliness (self-generated unrighteousness, holes of nothingness in created reality).

6. <u>Argument Conclusion</u>. *Therefore*, if God creates anything at all, it can *only* be distinct from God, less-than absolutely perfect, and inevitably be prone to self-generated fallenness and sin.

So, just by God creating *anything at all*, just by that act of creation, what is created, by God, *can only be not absolutely perfect*, and by that fact anything created by God will be prone to succumb to having aspects that are internally caused, self-caused (not God-caused)[23], as being against God, and thus of fallenness and sin.

The Bible is very clear in not ever stating that what God creates or created in the past is perfect. Rather, the Bible says what God creates is *good* (for example, Genesis 1:31). The Bible would contradict if it informed us that the

---

[23] In this book I will refer to the unGodliness attracting on itself and collapsing into sin, where I will call that happening an internal causation, or self-causation, but it may, in fact, be a sort of anti-causation, or reverse-causation, wherein reality has a hole ripped into it, in a "generation of nothingness" (no-thing-ness). God is the creator of all things, so sin must be a non-thing (nothing), like a void in reality, or the creation of a hole, a rip of nothingness, in reality.

perfect God created perfect creations, where the one Perfect created other non-identical and singular Perfects. 2 Tim. 3:17 discusses how man will be perfected in the future, which is the subject of the next chapter, where we will see that pure logic leads to that conclusion.

3. Logic of Reality Unveils a God-as-Redeemer Ontology

Logic will bring us, in this chapter, to elegant resolutions and descriptions of some of the biggest theological mysteries and questions of all. The answers are discoverable in the simple logic, that follows from proof for the existence of God (YHVH) discussed in Chapter 1, and by simple findings that emerge from that proof, which reveal a theo-*logical* fabric to the rudimentary nature of existence, of any reality that God creates. The revealing way reality is found, in this chapter, to be created-and-structured logically would be more indication of how God has put His signature into His created reality for created human beings to unveil, to discover Him by, and for that very reason to transcend the created realm in order to look at Him all the time, meditate on Him in prayer, and to celebrate His Being that is revealed by *penetrating past* the physical reality we can see, to therein see the unseen omnipresent One, the Maker, and who is Light everywhere (this is the topic of nonphysical Calvinism of Part 3 below). But we don't celebrate in the world—in the forests and cities—rather, we celebrate in the Heavens, with Him, now, before our physical bodies die—where the logic God built into His creation is one of our greatest tools for finding this life of celebration in God-Christ. Just like when the Creator-Logos revealed Himself with miracles when He walked the earth in the Holy Land, so too, His creation omnipresently contains His stamp, uncovered with pure logical deductions, starting from the most sure knowledge we have.

In this chapter, we will definitively discover what evil is (it is not identical so sin), how and why God creates evil (Isaiah 45:7), why and how God allows evil, pain, and sin to continue instead of stopping it all, and how God saves (redeems) His good-but-not perfected creation by unifying with it. In general, this chapter is a big-picture analysis that shows how the logic of our reality unveils why the reality is as it is, where our reality that is imperfect and damaged will be saved by its Creator.

Isaiah 45:7: God Creates Evil

The argument of the previous chapter that solves the problem of evil may shed light on the following widely discussed verse from Isaiah in the in the KJV:

> Isaiah 45:7 King James Version (KJV)
>
> 7 I form the light, and create darkness: I make peace, and create evil: I the Lord do all these things.

This is not the only verse in the Old Testament that says that God created and creates evil. This is a highly avoided issue among Christians, and it is certainly one that needs to be understood. And by understanding it, we can greatly further the understanding of our function as beings in a physical realm, versus as beings existing in Christ.

Typically, Christians equate sin and evil, as if they are synonyms, but they cannot be, since God creates evil, but God cannot create sin. But then what is evil? And how can evil be a creation of God, as Isaiah 45:7 clearly states (and, again, it is by no means the only verse that mentions this in the Old Testament). To get an idea as to the answer, consider this verse:

2 Chronicles 29:6 King James Version (KJV)

6 For our fathers have trespassed, and done that which was evil in the eyes of the Lord our God, and have forsaken him, and have turned away their faces from the habitation of the Lord, and turned their backs.

So, what is evil?

Evil **(definition):** God creating and sustaining the existence of nonsalvific humans (unchosen[24] aspects of His creation), and God sustaining their self-existence while they conduct free-willed, worldly (non-Godly) actions that are the result of their choice[25] (their choice to have their minds to be fixed on creation and created things rather than on God). [26]

This will be explained in much more detail below. And this will become very important in our discussion of faith in Parts 2 and 3, where we will discuss how human action that is not of faith is sin, which we will deduce to mean: human action that is not in constant communion with God is sin. In 2

---

[24] How, *exactly*, a loving God can create some humans to be chosen for salvation and some not is a sticky issue with many, but that is a concept that is directly in the Word of God, and one that has a very clear explanation, where when one sees the reasons why, it is only logical that God created two sorts of humans souls that have been created: chosen and unchosen. See Grupp 2018b and 2018c for a detailed breakdown of the specific reasons.

[25] There is some debate among Calvinists as to if humans make choices of their own accord (which would be free-willed choices), or if God or Satan make all the choices through humans wherein humans are not actually free-willed. I hold the position that that humans *do* make free-willed choices, for many reasons, such as because of verses such as this, which appear to involve God commanding humans to make free-willed choices (to choose Him):

    Deuteronomy 30:19 King James Version (KJV)

    19 I call heaven and earth to record this day against you, that I have set before you life and death, blessing and cursing: therefore choose life, that both thou and thy seed may live.

[26] A more detailed definition of evil will be given in Chapter 10 below.

Chronicles 29:6, we see that evil is a state of human existence that the Lord observes, in viewing humans as ignoring Him to look at all that is left to look at: the creation. God allowing and sustaining their free-will selves that do evil (desire the not-Godly) is how the Lord *creates evil*, as discussed in Isaiah 45:7.

From Scripture, what is denoted by the word "evil", is having a specific type of awareness and knowledge, that comes by filling our minds with creation (created physical objects), rather than God. Notice the wording of this verse:

> Genesis 2:9 King James Version (KJV)

> 9 And out of the ground made the Lord God to grow every tree that is pleasant to the sight, and good for food; the tree of life also in the midst of the garden, and the tree of knowledge of good and evil.

The message is that the forbidden tree was an avenue of forbidden *knowledge*—of evil. They could have knowledge of evil, if they chose, but until then, they would not have this knowledge, they would not have evil, which is a mindset, and perception-awareness problem. It is as if sin is a product of humans having knowledge of evil, or in other words, *the mind-awareness of focusing attention on what is not God*, and on the created rather than the Creator. As we will see below, this leads to violating God's commands (sin) while in the evil mindset.

So, evil is a mindset, not a force, or an energy—it is not of creation, it is associated with the nothingness of sin that contaminates the human mind. The creation (the physical realm) is not evil; it is scared by sin, but otherwise it is fallen, and it is good. Evil is an action, a mindset *inside* the human inner-subjective nonphysical self. That is why so many verses in the Old

Testament say, "He did evil in the sight of the Lord." The story of Solomon is perhaps the most interesting in this regard.

King Solomon is a person who had direct experience of God, but nevertheless turned away later in line. 1 Kings 11:1-13 tells us how it was Solomon's obsession with women (part of the phwycal domain) that turned his eyes from God, to the world (which is the production of *evil*). God specifically warned Solomon about this (1 Kings 11:2), but in 1 Kings 11:4 we see that Solmon's heart turned from God, which is the turn to evil, and in 1 Kings 11:6 we find this verse:

> 1 Kings 11:6 New King James Version (NKJV)
>
> 6 Solomon did evil in the sight of the Lord, and did not fully follow the Lord, as did his father David.

So, the word "evil" refers to an *action*, in the human subjectivity, and it is the platform created by God (free willed consciousness) that sin is created from. We saw in Chapter 1 that the mind and its contents are creations of God, so if free will is one of those contents, and if that free will can be of evil (the platform of sin), then God creates evil

How can a human cross the line, going from the evil mindset to literally violation of God? Here is the answer:

> The world's works are imperfect, and humans acting in accord with the imperfect world (rather than of full surrender to God/Him), is *evil* (John 7:7), evil is not of God, and the human mind desiring the world's works, or evil, is to have the human's mind not of God. Actions that desire to not be of God will be actions that violate God's commands and ways (sin).

Merely by preoccupying over, fixating on, the world (the imperfect), rather than on the Creator, is doing evil, and living in the moment-to-moment experiencing of God. This leads to evil in the present world, as it also did before the Fall, where back then it led to the change where one has less similarities with, and closeness to, God after the Fall. When sin occurred, and contaminated reality by putting original sin[27] into all humans and disfiguring the rest of creation, the sin altered all people and made them like the imperfected and scarred creation (it made them like the world, worldly), since they were now far less similar to God, who is not sinful. *This is how by merely fixating on the world, evil was generated*, into sin, leading to the good-but-imperfection creation developing holes of sin-nothingness within it. In the Old Testament, over and over, story after story, we are told of people looking away from God and looking at the world, and thus doing evil in the sight of the Lord.

So, it's seemingly an automatic situation:

a. God creates the imperfect (the imperfect-good that is not God). God instructs humans to fix their eyes on Him.

b. God supports the existence of humans who chose to obsess over imperfect creation and that which is not-God.

c. Humans *desire* (Genesis 3:6) to be of the not-God ways.

d. Humans are corrupted by the imperfect experience of physical-nothingness, altering their minds.

---

[27] See Grupp 2018d for verification that original sin is a completely correct doctrine. Many question this view, but the reasons are absolutely Scriptural. However, I hold a somewhat supralapsarian view, and thus I hold that humans first were created and did not have original sin, wherein that contamination came later (namely, when sin happened via Adam and Eve). So, in a sense, I agree with both Eastern orthodox Christianity, and Western Protestantism, in how the former says we were not created with original sin, and the latter says (now) all humans have original sin. For reasons why I hold this view, see my introduction to fullness Calvinism in Grupp 2018c.

e. Humans do works of the imperfect (sin).

f. That which is a not God creation of God will self-create violations of God.

a leads to e, and the creation needs to be saved, redeemed. Here is a diagram of how the process works, and which, seemingly, is inevitable for any created reality by the perfect One:

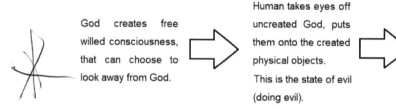

God creates free willed consciousness, that can choose to look away from God.

Human takes eyes off uncreated God, puts them onto the created physical objects. This is the state of evil (doing evil).

The Equation of how God creating evil leads to free willed sin creation.

By fixating on the physical realm, the human mind becomes infused by what it sees (the imperfect, rather than perfect uncreated God), and the mind is influenced by, takes after, what is sees (contradictory physical matter-nothingness [see Part 3]), which is *utterly different and diminished*, corrupted and imperfected, by comparison to the hyper-power of the holiness in the fear of the Lord-God.

Explanation of the First Sin (Satan's First Sin)

We can see this explicitly throughout the Bible, especially in the Old Testament. We see this with the first humans sin, Adam and Eve in Genesis 3, where Eve had *desire* for the fruit (lust for what is not God), where we are specifically told she sees it as *beautiful* (she is looking away from God, finding pleasure in what is not God, she is obtaining *knowledge* of good and evil by partaking of *that* tree), and she has *desire* for it (her mind was moved not by God, but by the physical, seeking fullness in a new, unGodly, imperfected item, down from the all-powerfulness of experience of God). There is (i) first the looking away from the uncreated God and at created objects (mind-state of evil), and then (ii) the desire comes in, that (iii) leads to sin (Genesis 3:6, James 1:14-15). Evil is the act of a human dwelling on the created, on what is imperfect and not-God, and thus knowledge of created things that are not of heaven when our minds are to be on heaven (Col. 3:1-2), wherein our lack of focus (lack of faith) on God, in God, _is sin_ (Rom. 14:23).

But Adam and Eve were the _second_ instance of sin in the Garden of Eden. Satan's sin was before that, which is an issue that has stumped theologians, especially Calvinists, who will typically say they have no explanation for how sin could emerge in a God's good creation. But we can see a simple explanation for it in the previous paragraphs, and in Ezekiel 28.

Satan was a spectacular angel, probably a seraphim, one of the closest to God. We know that Satan developed lust to be God, and to not be under Him. But look at this critically important passage, of God describing Satan:

> Ezekiel 28:15-17 New King James Version (NKJV)
>
> 15 You were perfect in your ways from the day you were created,
>
> Till iniquity was found in you.
>
> 16 "By the abundance of your trading
>
> You became filled with violence within,
>
> And you sinned;
>
> Therefore I cast you as a profane thing
>
> Out of the mountain of God;
>
> And I destroyed you, O covering cherub,
>
> From the midst of the fiery stones.

17 "Your heart was lifted up because of your beauty;

You corrupted your wisdom for the sake of your splendor;

I cast you to the ground,

I laid you before kings,

That they might gaze at you.

In verse 17 we see the specific key to the formula of how the free willed not-yet-sinned angel (Satan) being *becomes* a free willed sinner: "17 Your heart was lifted up because of your beauty; You corrupted your wisdom for the sake of your splendor..." Precisely in line with the formula above, Satan's gaze went *off* of the Lord, *onto* created being (his own beautiful being). Satan's body, his being, was created by God, to reside right next to God, and thus Satan was of unfathomable beauty, and in looking at his own being and body, obsessing over himself, rather than maintaining proper fixation on creator-God, *led to wrongly placed interests and desires (passion over the created rather than the Uncreated—which is the production of evil), and that is the avenue to sin, since Satan's mind would therein conform to the unGodly, imperfected interests of obsessing over what is lower than God, what is not God.* It is that awareness change, that interest shift, *from* uncreated God *to* created things, made possible by the free will that God creates and sustains in angels and humans, that led to misalignment with God, generating sin.

Notice that the passage says of Satan, "you were *perfect* in your *ways,*" and not "in your *being.*" Satan was not perfect in himself, but his actions were perfected for a time, as they would be with any being who God controls and operates thru (see John 14:10). This could be why Satan thought he could be like God, because his imperfected and beautiful being exhibited perfected actions. But, as we will see from what is written below, there are reasons that God cannot over-manage His creation, and therein make it too much like Himself (lest it will not be a genuinely distinct creation of God's), and God had to let Satan's free will (free will, itself, being a supernatural creation of God[28]) carry its course.

The Gravitational Model of Sin

Consider the part (i) of premise 4 of the above argument:

(i)   elements of unGodliness in the creation will inevitably interact, and by interacting will multiply their levels of unGodliness (I call this _the gravitation model of sin_, and I will break it down in the paragraphs below), and since

This involves what I call _the gravitation model of sin_. The model basically envisions sin as very much like the current academic model of gravitation, according to Big Bang Cosmology[29]. According to that model, gravity brings matter together, and the more that concentrated in one place, the more gravitation there is, where it can get to the point where gravitation will overcome all structure of matter in a region, which will have great ramifications to the matter around the region (such as attracting it inward

---

[28] See Grupp 2018a for more discussion of this concept of free will being a supernatural entity.

[29] By using the phrase "gravitational model of sin", I am not endorsing any particular model of cosmology, nor am I disregarding the ancient Hebrew model of cosmology. I am only using the phrase because sin, from my observations, works as a remarkable analogy when compared to the mechanics of gravitation according to the theoretical model of gravitation in professional theoretical science. Otherwise, there is no connection to Big Bang Cosmology and this book.

onto itself). Sin acts very much like this. It is as if gravitation represents evil, astrophysical bodies represent the matter objects in our world, and sin is gravitational collapse, where the inevitable outcomes are breakdown (collapse) of the self in sin. The world entices, causes desire over it, and leads to inevitable sin. From my observations of the world, hatred fuels more hatred, violence more violence, sin grows as it mixes, and it churns in the world. For example, in Genesis 6:5, not long after God had created the world, that the chaos of sin had escalated to such a point that we find the following written:

> Genesis 6:5 King James Version (KJV)
>
> 5 And God saw that the wickedness of man was great in the earth, and that every imagination of the thoughts of his heart was only evil continually.

So, it is safe to conclude that evil bunches up and concentrates, where observationally we see results in collapses into in reality (sin, or holes in reality).

Analogous to the theory of gravitation, singularities of unGodliness (sin) that inevitably develop are imperfect regions that develop corruption, blemish, and not-Godly *concentration-regions* in the creation (such as in Eve's mind, in the case of our specific universe-reality) that are unrighteousness (thus no longer being creations of God, zones of sin-nothingness[30]). Matter collapses on itself via its intense concentrations, and the gravitational collapse of a black hole is like sin creating a hole in reality, where eventually the collapses happen all over, glutting the reality in some places.

---

[30] God creates all things, and since sin is not a creation of God, it must be a no-thing (nothingness), like a hole in reality, so to speak. James 1:14-15 are relevant to some of the fine-details of this premise of the argument (such as the developing of sin into fullness of sin).

There is Only One _Perfect_

Notice that premise 1 in the argument involves a strong case for the idea that only monotheism can be true, as there can only be _one_ perfect Being, just as would be expected from our findings in Chapter 1, that the perfect Being is the God of the Bible (YHVH).[31]

By use of the word "imperfect," typically a person reading that believes there is a negative connotation involved. I only mean by the use of this word to refer to that which is not God, but created by Him. So, the imperfect, not-God creation, is _good_, however unGodly. God, in creating entities distinct from Himself, can only create entities that are _good_, even if they are less than perfect: an infinite God can only create what is good, since it would be is impossible that the infinite Creator (YHVH/God) of all, who has created our inner minds, our selves, to make a mistake[32] and create something not good.

Note that this argument above does not, necessarily, mean _all_ of creation is not good. The above argument does not infer that conclusion, and we know

---

[31] There are many ramifications to this, such as, for example, how many atheists often claim that Christianity is tritheism, not monotheism, but where tritheism is logically impossible, since there cannot be three absolutely perfect beings with non-identical haecceities. There can be only one perfect, since perfect cannot be added to, to make it "more perfect"—if it could be made "more perfect" it would not have been perfect in the first place. This is why God/Trinity (Father, Son, Spirit) can only be _one_:

    1 John 5:7 King James Version (KJV)

    7 For there are three that bear record in heaven, the Father, the Word, and the Holy Ghost: and these three are one.

[32] Notice that this point, which seems to be inescapable, contradicts the widely held Christian view that the Fall of Creation was an accidental event, in some way, where God took a risk, as it's often said, created humans and _whoops!_, they sinned. I find that view, however, entirely non-Biblical, and non-logical (because it does not follow the logic of this chapter), since there are verses that tell how the Cross was pre-planned before Creation (Acts 4:26-28, Acts 2:23), which would indicate that God (obviously) knew from the beginning that sin would enter the world:

    Acts 2:23 New International Version (NIV)

    23 This man was handed over to you by God's deliberate plan and foreknowledge; and you, with the help of wicked men, put him to death by nailing him to the cross.

that creation—other than the locations of the holes of nothingness (namely inside human minds, see Grupp 2018a)—is good, and remained imperfect-but-good after the fall (1 Tim. 4:4).

Problem of Evil Solved Argument in Shorter Form

The above argument can be presented in the following extremely terse manner, for purposes of ministry, as follows:

> If God creates anything it has to be distinct from Him,
>
> And can only be imperfect.
>
> What is imperfect will contain (self-develop) qualities of imperfection (like sin and pain).
>
> And for that reason, anything God creates will develop inside of itself, pain and sin, and will need to be redeemed.

But an even *quicker* version of the argument, if needed in ministry, is as follows:

> What a *perfect* God creates is different from Him and is thus not *perfect*, and thus will contain imperfection and ultimately corruption.

That form of the argument can be presented in about 10 seconds, if not 5 or 6 seconds, to any person during the ministry setting, a short-enough time interval to prevent interruptions. The argument is simple enough that it will likely not be derailed by questions before the 5-10 seconds is over. The simplicity of the argument, and the Biblical adherence, will likely not lead to many further questions, if any at all, and ministry can merely move on to the good news of the free gift of the grace of Jesus Christ. My experience has been that some I talk to are just amazed at how what has been written above answers the long-standing issue of the problem of evil in such a tidy and definitive manner, and in a way that shows the answer is just built into the nature of created reality.

Why God Allows Pain and Sin to Continue

The solution to the problem of evil, and the problem of pain, just unveiled, contain the disclosure that anything the One/Perfect (YHVH) creates can only exist in one of three states:

a. Pre-fallen:

Reality created by God, that is not absolutely perfect, but is *good*, and has not yet been internally self-corrupted as to where it contains the self-created internal patches of unrighteous nothingness (sin).

b. Fallen:

Independently of the Creator, imperfect created reality *self-generates* in specific regions (in the case of our universe, this was in the consciousness of Eve, where she had desire, in Genesis 3:6), where it develops cracks or holes of unrighteousness (sin), and thus are not of God, and thus can no longer exist. These are patches of Creation that have lost their righteousness, and thus are unrighteous zones of death. By such holes of nothingness in created reality, the rest of creation remains good (2 Tim. 4:4), but nevertheless out to its borders becomes contaminated with scarification from this damage (which is sin contamination),

c. Redeemed:

That which has been created, and has obtained a status of alienation and/or separation from God, must be saved, redeemed, by God, which means that God must make sin-corrupted reality again like Him, in His likeness, so it can again exist and escape being blotted out (see Heb. 2:17).

Presumably there could be realities that God creates that remain in stage a, unlike ours which went from stage a to stage b (and which will soon go to c), but this would seem enormously unlikely, since (1) what is not-God should only spontaneously originate internally and self-caused fallenness, and since (2) God is a *redeemer*, a sacrifice of love (see Chapter 4), and His love needs to serve as a maximal *sacrifice of grace* to any reality that is created, wherein reality would need to be *fallen*, and filled with holes of nothingness, in order for God to *be what He is*: a pure infinite sacrifice and redeemer.

One may still wonder why God would not at least *stop* evil and pain, even if such prevention was needed quite regularly, or all the time, in order to keep the creation from spiraling into self-decay. If He is an infinite God that can do all things, couldn't He do *that*, and do it at all times?

The Bible is clear that God is quite actively involved in doing continual corrections to His creation: intervening specifically to *change* (make more Godly) some events, and to prevent and bring about other events He chooses, according to His perfect ways. One of the most dominant themes in the Bible is God's active control and management of His creation.

If God prevented *all* evil, painful, sinful, and harmful events, preventing them from happening, then the creation would start to resemble a *perfected* reality, it would not operate in the way it normally would in-itself as an imperfect reality, and in ways would therefore not represent a genuinely *distinct* creation of God's, different than God.

So how does God decide which sinful and pain-causing events are to be allowed, that He will *not* prevent? It would appear that the answer is: the events that would make the creation perfected, or perhaps parts of it perfected, so they are not genuinely distinct creations of God. And for that reason, God will have to allow creation to go on imperfected and with holes of sin-nothingness, only shaping and molding the creation, not perfecting it. These points made in this section are an answer to the long-standing question of why God would allow sin and pain to exist without preventing all of it—without preventing more of the pain and sin in addition to the pain and sin He is *already* preventing. This is how God is in control of all things: He allows some pain, evil, and sin proceed, so as not to correct the creation to the point of making it indistinguishable from Himself, and that *allowing* represents how He is still in control of all things. If God is to save the entire creation, out of what is savable and redeemable, a different, and gradual operation is needed, and for putting His perfection into it, as we will explore shortly.

How to Fix Imperfect, Sin-Ridden Reality: Coinherence (Co-indwelling) with God and His Perfection

But the most important question is: after the imperfect-but-good creation is created, and inevitable holes of nothingness arise within it, is there any way that God can alter, redeem, or liberate the creation so that it can be fixed without perpetually existing in the out-of-control prison of internal-impalement (internally caused sin)? I think there is an overwhelmingly obvious answer to that question: an imperfect-but-good creation *must have perfection*, being of or like God, in some way, to avoid the inevitable problems of imperfection leading to evil. There is no other way around it.

But of course, as we just saw, problems emerge when we theorize a solution that involves God over-managing His creation, which has the effect of blotting out His creation, since it would not be a *distinct* creation, and would just be more of God. *But*, if instead, parts of the creation, of its own accord, self-altered in order to become like God (specifically by becoming sacrifices, just like God is a sacrifice—which is the subject of the Chapter 4), offering their haecceities, their essences, to God, to be to-the-core servants to God, but all without destroying their haecceities, since it is a *self-giving*, and thus remaining a *distinct* creation of God's, *that* would lead to a creation that was perfected but still a distinct creation, and that would allow a creation to be saved from the inevitable self-degeneration prison that is involved in being an imperfect creation (a creation distinct from God). What has been written in this paragraph is the key to understanding that the logic of reality—of the reality created by God (YHVH)—involves *a redemption ontology*, where if God chooses to redeem and liberate humanity He can do so. And being a Being of perfect love, grace, and sacrifice, He will do what a human cannot understand or have the capacity to do, which is *be an infinite sacrifice* (the subjects of the next chapter). Pure logic leads to these conclusions, as we will see, in a simple and elegant fashion.

As was just mentioned, the only solution here is for the imperfect created beings to keep their haecceities, but otherwise reject their own existences and by their own nature and volition, become fully owned and controlled by God, and in *that* way perfected. If the created being does this, instead of it only being God that is reaching out for this unification that saves the imperfected creation from its doom-of-imperfection, the created being also will need to use its volition to mix its being with the Creator, *to give its full control to the Creator*, therefore altering its nature, *from* of the imperfect *to* being possessed by the Perfect, losing its imperfected self-control, keeping its haecceity while becoming fully new. It would have to be that the created being, of its own nature, becomes like God, like the Perfect, rather than only by-way of God imposing His way into the created being. God, being a Being of infinite love, is always reaching out maximally to humanity as much as He can without over-intruding, over-managing with His nature into created reality so as to overpower it and eliminate its distinctness, making it equal to Himself, so, *created being must also contribute, reach back, so the two can mix, coinhere, become unified, where again the human can be a slave to God.*

John 15:5 King James Version (KJV)

5 I am the vine, ye are the branches: He that abideth in me, and I in him, the same bringeth forth much fruit: for without me ye can do nothing.

How Can a Created Being, Who Can't See God, Become a Self-Sacrifice to God?

So, the simple logic of reality confirms that there is a creator-God who is YHVH (Ch.1), who can only create realities that are good-but-imperfect, become damaged, and need to be redeemed (Ch. 2), where created beings become evil by obsession with created being rather than Creator, and the way for God to save reality is for created beings to sacrifice their lives to already maximally sacrificing-loving Creator I AM that I AM. So, this brings us to a huge dilemma: How can imperfect created beings reach out to the Perfect via their own volition and free-will? This is why free will exists: for the imperfect created beings to be atoned in the perfect God-Christ-Holy Spirit. This is why God created beings with free will at the *outset* of creation:

> God knew the conscious beings of His creation would fall into sin-nothingness, and therefore would need a way out of it. So, in creating the free-will consciousness some of His creations possess (such as humans), God created the avenue for evil, in addition to salvation.

A major problem is that the contaminated created beings do not have the capacity to use their free will to sacrifice their lives to their creator-God, and to be like their sacrificially loving God, since the created beings, in being damaged by evil and sin, have adopted the properties of the world, which are opposite properties of God. The ways of God are such that we are to be *owned by others* (which is the opposite of the way that the world—culture—thinks), enslaved in love and service to others (see Romans 12:5), where in creation the created beings are to be owned by each other as they are slaves to their God (recall Paul discussing in many places being a "slave for

Christ!"), not self-owned (not _selfish_). Earlier in this chapter, we saw how the fixation on the world (on the worldly), rather than on God, generated evil—as illustrated all through the Old Testament—which caused the human to be less like God, to be sinful, therein fascinated with, and locked-onto, the worldly, acting in ways opposite of God, such as being egotistical, self-interested, and with preoccupations on self, rather than God's ways, which is to be preoccupied with others, via perfected love. So, our problem is: How can the fully selfish created being become a full sacrifice to God? It is unclear how the self, which cannot see clearly, since it cannot see the ways of God, since it has become contaminated, a self that is acting in ways, and with interests, opposite of God (such as acting according to its own fears and desires), which _blind_ the created being, seemingly barring the created being from experiencing God's ways, or recognizing Him in reality outside of the egotistical self, and therefore unaware of Truth, endlessly living in and creating self-contradictory agendas, ways of life, and ideologies.

It seems the only way created beings could sacrifice their lives to the Perfect (YHVH), is if the created being lost all self-seeking, self-preservation, wanted to abandon itself, in order to reject its own existence to splice its existence with God's. But how would that happen? But how could there be any way that a creation of God's, an imperfect creation which may have been _good_ at one point, but which does not know perfection, has never known it, cannot even imagine it, of its own accord become just like the Perfect, without losing its self-haecceity, its specific _I am_? The answer is: _it can't_.

It could only be that the creator-God would have to _draw_ and _entice_ the sinful, damaged, created being _to Him_, whereby of the created being's own accord the created being would be pulled out of the imperfect domain, and become a devoted sacrifice to the Perfect. It would appear that this is the way the mechanics of reality must work, and if one deconstructs reality to its fine rudiments, these mechanics are what is left: the Biblical ontology is the rudimentary logic of reality, stemming from *cogito ergo sum*.

John 6:44

To be pulled outside its life, its self, its existence, the created being would have to see and comprehend, to some degree, Power beyond the ways of the realm of imperfection, and this drawing, pulling, revealing, would need to have the effect of transforming the imperfect self from recognizing only the imperfect to having some awareness of what the Perfect is all about. Again, this would require the mindset of the imperfect created being to be *changed* at the point of beholding, to some degree, of the Perfect/Godly: the imperfect created being would have to go outside of its self-interest, against its innate ways of not being like God, and being blinded by self, to see another aspect of reality on terms not immediately familiar to the self, to comprehend that it has seen something that does not fit the realm of the imperfect, realizing that deductively they have witnessed something outside of the realm of the imperfect, and have interest in it, to the point of possibly sacrificing their lives to it. How could the blinded self see outside of itself to notice God's signs? Answer: because the human is in God's image, *he is a spirit* (Chapter 1), and the human created being cannot get away from his self. So, some will see, some will recognize, some will awaken from their sin-sleep, when they behold an act of God (miracle) that is meant to draw them to God.

This pulling, drawing, should be quite possible for *some* of the created beings, since, as we saw in Chapter 1, the created beings are made in the image of the Spirit they were created: just by being created by a nonphysical Spirit, created beings, such as humans, will have resemblance to God (YHVH), and some will be aware of their inner being as resembling a miracle seen by God: they should recognize from the true nature of their inner cores that have the Kingdom of God within them (Luke 17:21), to varying degrees, a reality greater than the imperfect, and should be able to recognize the Perfected. It is by these dynamics that some of the created beings can be drawn to God.

So, the Creator would have to present Himself as purely in the context and terms of the created, where created beings could experience the works and ways of the Creator, in a way recognizable to the created beings, whereby some will be able to notice the perfected Power that exists outside of the imperfect order of things.

The question is: How can a corrupted created being be so overtaken by a vision, a sign, a miracle of the Creator, that the created being will sacrifice its life to the creator-God? The Lord presents Himself to all people (Romans 1:20-21), but only *some* are structured as to where they can to be chosen (what is meant by this will be investigated in detail in Part 3, also see Grupp 2018b and 2018c). Those who are changed by beholding God will gain the capacity to make a free will choice, caused by the verification of the perfect Creator, where before that they did not have the capacity to make that free willed choice. Only *some* make the free willed choice for God, to the point of becoming salvific. It is as if the Creator is a magnet, humans are a mix of sand grains and iron shavings, and the Creator glides over the top of the mix, pulling out the iron shavings, pulling out those that are drawn to Him. And why it's only *some*, rather than all, who are pulled, I discussed in copious detail elsewhere (see Grupp 2018b, 2018c).

Some humans hang on to self and self-interest more than others, and are more blinded than others, just by their innate structure and makeup as personae.[33] That group has more difficulty seeing beyond the self and its fears and desires. And the more a person is anchored in evil (fixation on world) and self-preservation, the less connected to God they are, and the less likely they are to recognize a sign from God, due to their blindness (think of the Pharisees, who in response to a miracle of Jesus, were not amazed but had their hearts further hardened).

For those who are more interested in the sign from the Spirit that they see, those created beings will move *to the Creator*, choose the Creator, preserving their haecceity, but emptied of self's contents, to be filled with the Creator's perfection. This would lead to the created entity as being entirely of a new form that it had not previously had (now a filled vessel, see Part 3), being perfect like the Father in Heaven is perfect (since the Father-God is now the power of the vessel of the created being). In this way, God can save the imperfect creation.

Any creation of God must be redeemed in this way. A created reality, any creation of God, must be *of God*, not of itself, in order to indeed be perfect, to not self-generate unGodliness, and thus in order to stay in existence. God

---

[33] That there are specific templates to what people are like, almost like mathematical codes and templates, like a mold a potter has shaped, is what I argued in Grupp 2018b is the key to understanding the Biblical view of a human, and which answers all sorts of theological cruxes. This issue will come up again in Part 3 below.

must be put back in control, to reserve and/or make new the problems and damage.

> *The created entity becomes a sacrifice, its being becomes sacrificial being, where it voluntarily, of its self-existence, it donates its existence to God, wherein God is to become the owner and controller.*

This logic is a portrait of Christian theology, and the pure logic up to this point leads us to Christian Biblical ontology as being the description of the logical base of existence—seemingly any reality that can exist.

This act of sacrificial interconnection is initiated by God, since He is already in a state of sacrificial love, as we will explore in the next chapter, and the creation must of its own accord allow and not block the incoming control from Creator-God. This would appear to be a description of the logic of Christian ontology, built into the substratum of created reality, where God pulls the person to Him, and where that is the only way a person can be redeemed (John 6:44).

Nothing but simple reason and logic has been used so far. If we start at the most rudimentary base-point of reality (*I think therefore I am*), with the cleanest of logic we end up right where we are:

1. *Cogito ergo sum.*
2. Reality is created by a Perfect Being (YHVH) (Chapter 1).
3. Created reality is distinct from the Perfect (Chapter 2).
4. God had to create what He is not.
5. God creates free willed minds and sustains them, to give them an escape from imperfect and sinful/painful reality.

6. The free willed minds generate evil, God sustains them through this (Isaiah 45:7 KJ V).

7. Reality is imperfect and now has holes of sin (Chapter 2).

8. Evil and sin overruns created imperfect reality.

9. God must allow pain and evil to not be fully eradicated lest creation cease to be distinct from Him (God can't overmanage reality).

10. Created beings must coinhere with God to escape, be saved, the inevitable impaled nature of created reality.

11. To coinhere, created beings who don't know perfection must forgo self and give all to God to be His perfection.

12. God pulls created beings to lure them into free willed coinherence.

These are the steps we've taken so far in this book. They are simple steps. All from pure logic, and all spelled-out completely. The Bible is a book of pure logic, written by Infinite Love (God), which is a mystery to men (Col. 2), since it is too large for them to understand. The Bible is the true scientific textbook of reality, the true engineering schematic that explains everything, but men rely on their own understanding, rather than on the mind of God.

Works Cited

Grupp, J eff, 2018a, "Sin, Nothingness, the Liar Paradox, and the Contamination of Creation," in *Theologic: Revelation, Calvinism, Surrender, Nothingness*, Kalamazoo: Praise and Love Church, pages 32-54 print copy available at Lulu Books.

Grupp, Jeff, 2018b, "God's Pre-Election Knowledge of the Soul: A New Interpretation of Biblical Election and Predestination Showing Why God Only Chose Some Rather Than All," in _Theologic: Revelation, Calvinism, Surrender, Nothingness_, Kalamazoo: Praise and Love Church, pages 5-31, (print copy available at Lulu.com, free online copy at Praiseandlove.net).

Grupp, Jeff, 2018a, Dec. 31, "Fullness Calvinism: Expanding Calvinist Theology to Resolve Big Theological Puzzles", YouTube Channel: Praise and Love, URL: https://www.youtube.com/watch?v=-LhIi8ZhjWM.

Grupp, Jeff, 2018d, "Proof That the Doctrine of Original Sin is Scriptural Truth," in _Theologic: Revelation, Calvinism, Surrender, Nothingness_, Kalamazoo: Praise and Love Church, pages 121-123, (print copy available at Lulu.com, free online copy at Praiseandlove.net).

4. A New Proof for the Existence of the God of the Bible: A Monotheistic Creator-God Can Only Be An Infinite Sacrifice

Introduction

In this chapter I will show that the creator-God *can only be a God of infinite sacrificial love*, and therefore can only be the Christian God of the Bible. The findings of this chapter follow from the previous chapter, which involved logical findings for how God can only create a universe that, while initially is only good, will inevitably self-generate evil and pain, for seemingly most (or all) universes and realities created by God. Also like the previous chapter, the findings of this chapter—that the only possible creator-God that can exist for any reality, as the necessary cause for any reality that can possibly exist, *is a God of infinite sacrificial love* (that is, Jesus Christ, the divine indwelling Logos)—is built into the logical structure of reality. In other words.

I consider this chapter the most powerful and important chapter of this book, since, in building on the findings of the previous two chapters, the conclusions of this chapter would appear to prove, to a startlingly degree, and in astonishingly simple fashion, what is in the title of this part of the book: *if anything whatsoever exists, it can only be that it is a creation of the God of the Bible.* It would appear, as spelled-out below, that the simple logic of reality leads directly to that conclusion, and always has, but men apparently have not seen it.

I have found these arguments of indispensable aid in ministry settings that involve debate with even the most impressively intellectual atheists and academics, who I have found defenseless against the points given in this chapter, and much of this book.

The logical arguments up to and thru this chapter lead to the development of new logic that describes our reason for being here in this world (which is that we are creations of God, for God, meant to live in God's holiness and holy light).

1 Peter 2:9 New International Version (NIV)

9 But you are a chosen people, a royal priesthood, a holy nation, God's special possession, that you may declare the praises of him who called you out of darkness into his wonderful light.

Proof that the Creator-God Can Only be Infinite Love

There are four logical arguments presented in this chapter. Here is the first argument, which I call *The God is Infinite Sacrificial Love Argument*:

1. God is infinite (Psalm 147:5 KJ V).
2. What God creates will always and only be less than the absolute perfection of God (subject of Chapter 2).
3. God, being the one perfect Being, need not create anything, since He is perfectly complete as He is, and since nothing can be added to God, the one perfect Being (Eccl. 3:14)

4. Since God cannot gain anything, have anything added in, God creates everything *solely for the other* (for what He creates): He creates *only* for the benefit of what is non-God (for that which is created).

5. To act solely for another, gaining nothing in return, is the definition of a pure sacrifice.

6. To be a pure sacrifice is to act in love.

7. <u>Conclusion 1</u>: In creating, since infinite God gains nothing, only creating for the benefit of the other that the created that is less than Him, then *God creates only via pure, infinite sacrificial love.*

It is as if the conclusion of *The God is Infinite Sacrificial Love Argument* is an undeniable finding, coming right from the logic of created reality.

And consider the next argument, which utilizes the unavoidable conclusion of the *God is Infinite Sacrificial Love Argument*, and which is an argument that I call *The God is Infinite Sacrificial Grace Argument*:

1. Since nothing can be added to God, the infinite sacrificial love from God *is one-way*: *from* creator-God *to* human (or to any other created entity).

2. There is nothing any created entity (such as a human person) can do to cause God to do His creating; God is the sole reason and the impetus for the creation of any entity that exists (this comes from the *God is Infinite Sacrificial Love Argument*)

3. (From 1) The infinite sacrificial love of the creator-God is *freely given* to a person, or any created entity, due to the blessing of being created by the creator-God, and thus being the recipient of the infinite sacrificial love.

4. God sustains all things, all of Creation, from moment-to-moment, including all people (Heb. 1:3).[34]

5. <u>Conclusion 2</u>: The creator-God continuously creates (at every moment) all of reality via a free gift of unearned infinite love, and He is the sole impetus and source of unearned infinite sacrificial love that is the fuel and reason for all of reality.

The logic of the two arguments so-far given in this chapter involve the fact that these findings (conclusions 1 and 2) seem to be the only way *any* reality can be:

The only way <u>anything</u> can exist—whether one atom, or a person, or a spirit, or a set of universes—is to be created by infinite, unfathomable, beatific, overjoyed, unwarranted, sacrificial love that comes from the creator-God. (In theological terms, this is the ekstasis of God, the ecstasy of God.[35])

God is perfectly complete, nothing can be added to Him, so in creating anything, the created entity that is created into existence does so *ex nihilo*, due to the fact that the created entity is *distinct* from God, and thus cannot come from God's being (or the *created* being would be perfect, and thus

---

[34] The atheist may object to this point, claiming that it is a Scriptural point, not a scientific or logical point. But there are multiple reasons for maintaining this point without referring to the Bible, such as the findings in Chapter 8 below when studying the implantation argument for the existence God, where it is shown that all atoms composing reality (partless philosophical atoms), on any scenario, must be created by a creator-God. This is true, to repeat, of any of the different models for what the partless atoms of that physical reality reduces to might be like (if they are eternal, if they flash in-and-out of existence, and so on). As seen in Chapter 8, a creator-God is needed to create all moments of the existence of the atoms. For this reason, this premise (premise 2) is verified, since if a creator-God is needed to create atoms, then the creator-God is needed to create *anything* in observable reality, since anything in physical reality is atoms. For those who believe in atomless reality (infinite divisibility, 'atomless gunk'), see the discussion in Chapter 8 on that topic, where it was found that that position reduces to point-atomism.
[35] The topic of the creation(s) of God as being products of His infinite ecstasy (*ekstatis*), God's creating selflessly in ecstatic love, was a dominant theme of the 6th C. Byzantine monk, Maximus the Confessor. Maximus has been gaining significant attention over the past 200 years by theologians.

would be God, rather than a separate creation—it would, in fact, not be a creation). For those reasons, God creates any created being that is distinct from Him *from nothing*, and none of this was earned by the created being, none of it deserved. It is solely a product of God's love. There is nothing a created entity can contain or involve to add anything to God after the created entity is created, to make Him more complete, to make Him in any way other than He is. There is nothing a created being has done to earn being created, as the created being is continuously created from moment to moment.

Maximal sacrificial love is when a person fully gives their entire being for another, even and especially if the other does not deserve it. The only way the creator-God can be in His creating of any reality, is to do so as a total sacrifice, as infinite love. All we see around us—the forest, the living forms, the sky, our minds, and so forth, are all only the product of the infinite love of God, and the logic of the arguments just given prove this deductively. The mechanics of anything that exists, of any reality, can only be a flux of dependent/created existence coming from nothing by the infinite love of God.

And God will *only* create. It appears that God will only be in an active state of *creating*—that's simply what He does, for eternity. I say this due to the following argument, which I call *The God is the Creator of Infinite Realities Argument:*

1. God is unchanging.
2. God increases (John 3:30).
3. God is unchangingly increasing (He exists at a constant and unchanging rate of increase) (from 1 and 2), and since He is already

infinite and nothing can be added to Him, He increases as an infinite does without being more thru the increase.[36]

4. Out of the overflow of the heart the mouth speaks (Matt. 12:34).

5. Conclusion 2 above: God is infinite love.

6. God creates all things (Rev. 4:11, Col. 1:16-17).

7. God *speaks* all things into existence (Psalm 33:5-9, Gen. 1).

8. If God continually creates from everlasting to everlasting, then there can only be infinite things He has created, and He will create infinitely *more* things.

9. Conclusion 3: God's overflowing, increasing heart evokes Him to endlessly speak all things into existence throughout eternity, creating all the infinite worlds, infinite beings, and infinite universes and all things within them.[37]

Conclusion 3 shows that it appears impossible for God *not* to be creating, since His heart is always overflowing, thus always speaking, and thus only *creating*—for eternity. This would indicate that that's *just what God does*, that's what He's been doing forever into the past, and will continue to forever into the future. Reality is in a state of *increasing*, where more and more reality is coming into existence, since God's heart is always overflowing.

---

[36] This is a very basic mathematical principle: if there is an infinite set of items, adding another item to the set does not change that the set is infinite. Items can continually be added to the set (a constant rate of increase) without changing that the set is infinite. Cantorian mathematics involves infinities increasing, since one infinite set can have infinitely more members than another infinite set. In that case, and if one wants to consider the mathematical infinity of God to that level, it would seem that God mathematical infinity clearly would be an infinite quantity that is identical to all the infinite sets combined.

[37] This is the very same conclusion I came to in my book *Theologic*, but in that book I came to that conclusion from an entirely different direction, and different set of premises. See Grupp 2018b, page 21-22. The conclusion of this argument I think fits best with a modal realist interpretation, following David Lewis's book, *On The Plurality of Worlds*, since I view reality as nonspatial (see Part 3).

Proof that the Creator God can Only be the Christian God

At the very end of Chapter 1 we saw new evidence that the Creator of reality is the God of the Bible. Conclusions 1 – 3 are not about just *any* God, but specifically about the Christian God, since it is the Christian God, the God of the Cross, who is the infinite sacrifice of infinite love. Consider the following argument, which also shows that:

1. Conclusion of previous chapter: *Therefore*, if God creates anything at all, it can *only* be distinct from God, less-than absolutely perfect, and inevitably be prone to self-generated fallenness and sin.

2. In our universe, the self-contamination of evil, of nothingness[38], has self-generated at a specific place: inside human minds.[39]

3. The creator-God can only respond to evil that has self-generated to create holes of nothingness in His creation as an infinite sacrifice.[40]

---

[38] See Grupp 2018c, and Sproul, RC, YouTube Channel, Idea Pump, Oct. 27, 2013, "What Is Evil & Where Did It Come From? - RC Sproul", YouTube.com, https://www.youtube.com/watch?v=5Ir6pKEV0RQ.

[39] See Grupp 2018c for discussion of the inner nothingness of sin that exists in human souls. All things are created by God, but this self-generation of sin is not included in "all things", since sin is nothingness.

[40] Psalm 5:5, and a few other verses in the Bible, talk about God *hating* sinners. But we have seen above that God can only be a God of love, as the Bible also states. God's name is *Love*. It must be the case that with the wrath of God, which also can only be love, can be interpreted and described by a human as hate or resentment, due to lack of understanding the infinity of the ways of God, and human language consequently falling short. But since God is infinite, and man is less than God's infinity, there is no question that the love of God that is recorded as hatred by David in Psalm 5:5 is described that way, as hate, because there are gaps in how our language can capture and describe the ways of infinite God. This is roughly like where there is an unsolved mathematics problem, M, and one person, person A, has solved part of it, and another person, person B, has worked on another part and solved that part, but the entirety of problem M is not solved, and therefore the full nature of problem M is out of the conscious range of person A and person B. But add to this that person A and person B have conflicting information in their partial solutions of M, in a way where A and B's solutions could be interpreted as contradicting each other, but where in reality A and B are each only seeing a non-complete picture of the solution of the entire problem, M, since the mathematics problem M lies beyond a full range of understanding by A and B, and if the entire problem was seen, and was not behind the veil of unknowing, of mystery, it would be seen that the conflict was only due to the partial nature of the solutions of A and B. if God's wrath, part of the infinity of God as one of His attributes, represents the entire mathematical solution, M, and A's and B's incomplete but partial solutions are A=God is Love, and B=God hates sin or sinners, if the entire infinite scope of God's wrath were known it would, I propose, be revealed that the apparent conflict of A and B is only due to having a partial view of God by each A and B.

4. If God responds to evil by offering Himself as an infinite sacrifice, the creator-God *will give the entirety of His being to them, as an infinite sacrifice*

5. God will only be able to reconcile Himself with the *entirety* of any and every aspect of His creation (see Col. 1:19-27), due to His being infinite perfect sacrifice of love to all He creates.

6. What has just been described is a description of the God of the Bible.

7. Conclusion 4: the only possible creator-God that can exist would be the God of the Bible.

The findings of Part 1 of this book all support this argument:

There is existence,

Therefore, the Christian God exists (as the cause).

From Chapter 1, by the most certain information there is (*cogito ergo sum*, or, I think therefore I am), we learned that there is a God, and it is the God of the Bible. And from the simplest logic, we derived all many pointed conclusions that reveal that from the most certain knowledge, we logically deduce the existence of a reality that is precisely, down to minute details (which cannot be a coincidence, or the result of some error on my part), show that reality as-a-whole is tightly in-line-with, the Christian ontological framework.

Works Cited:

Grupp, Jeff, 2018a, Dec. 31, "Fullness Calvinism: Expanding Calvinist Theology to Resolve Big Theological Puzzles", YouTube Channel: Praise and Love, URL: https://www.youtube.com/watch?v=-LhIi8ZhjWM.

Grupp, Jeff, 2018b, "God's Pre-Election Knowledge of the Soul: A New Interpretation of Biblical Election and Predestination Showing Why God Only Chose Some Rather Than All," in *Theologic: Revelation, Calvinism, Surrender, Nothingness*, Kalamazoo: Praise and Love Church, pages 5-31, (print copy available at Lulu.com, free online copy at Praiseandlove.net).

Grupp, Jeff, 2018c, "Sin, Nothingness, the Liar Paradox, and the Contamination of Creation," in *Theologic: Revelation, Calvinism, Surrender, Nothingness*, Kalamazoo: Praise and Love Church, pages 32-54 print copy available at Lulu Books.

Part 2: Debunking Atheism

In Part 1, the existence of the Christian God was proven using the absolute starting point the surest and most certain knowledge there is (Descartes' _cogito ergo sum_). Out of that, only the simplest of logic was used to conclude that the Christian God logically must exist if our reality is to exist, since the Biblical God's signature is in the logical fabric of reality. But some may ask: What about all the masses of scientists and professional academics, many of which are part of the largely growing atheist movement around the world, they have many brilliant people, whose claims are strong?

Next, in Part 2, I will take on atheism directly, where atheism will be solidly shown to not only be based on surprising simple errors, but furthermore, we will be able to look at the very core of atheism (which has three parts, which are the atheist's claims that there is evidence lacking for the existence of God, faith is a nonscientific and nonlogical concept, and the Bible is littered with absurdity and contradiction), and we will be able to soundly and swiftly show that the entire basis of atheism is based in simple _contradiction_—a true fatal blow to the thesis of atheism. This may be hard to believe, but we will come to these findings quite easily, the evidence is clear. Atheists just have had poor grasp on theology, and lack of any experience of God, apparently leading to the simple logical mistakes they have made.

The same attacks on Christianity that atheists often use are also often used by Islamicists, Satanists, scientologists, those of new age movements, and so on. The information in Part 2 can be expanded-out to give-rise to a very broad array of defense against non-Christian opposition. The reason this broad array exists, is simply because there is so much Christian opposition that is based on either bad information, or on poor knowledge of theology. For example, the definition of the concept of *faith* used by opponents of Christianity is seemingly almost always (1) belief without evidence, and/or (2) making the word "faith" synonymous with the word "belief", rather than understanding belief as an ingredient of faith (in fact, mainstream Christians very often make the second error, as well). I have seen the most prominent and influential atheists in the world make these errors. Both (1) and (2) are verifiably *incorrect*, and when opponents of Christianity have this pointed out to them, and also have it pointed out what the proper and accurate Biblical definition of "faith" is, it can furthermore be shown that their entire construct of anti-Christianism reduces to contradiction.

These two chapters in Part 2 are especially useful in many ministry settings where there is intelligent opposition: in situations where one is confronted by very intellectual atheists and anti-Christians, such as in debate with college professors, in street ministry, jail ministry, etc. But the chapters are in no way limited to that, and they contain fresh information not previously discussed anywhere else.

5. We Walk By *Faith*, Not By Sight: God is Not Found With Science

Key Verses

2 Corinthians 5:7 English Standard Version (ESV)

for we walk by faith, not by sight.

Hebrews 11:1 King James Version (KJV)

Now faith is the substance of things hoped for, the evidence of things not seen.

2 Corinthians 4:18 New International Version (NIV)

So we fix our eyes not on what is seen, but on what is unseen, since what is seen is temporary, but what is unseen is eternal.

Introduction

In this chapter, I will argue that the Bible on the one hand, and contemporary atheists on the other, are actually in *complete agreement* about the how much scientific, mathematical, or logical evidence there is for God—*which is precisely zero*—since God is found in *faith* in Jesus Christ ("We walk by faith, not by sight", 2 Cor. 5:7), and *not* found in empirical information (such as sight) or the intellectual systems and methods of humans. Christian faith is about *experiential evidence of the unseen* (Heb. 11:1 KJV), rather than about scientific and intellectual discovery.

But from what I can tell, it seems as if every atheist misses this point, surprisingly, and equally surprising it seems Christian theists often do also— where *each* side typically puts tremendous importance on whether or not there is scientific or logical evidence for God, but in doing this, they do not argue in the playing field of the Bible, *which specifically tells us we will not find God through science or intellectual analysis, but rather through direct revelation of God-Christ-Spirit*:

> John 6:44 New International Version (NIV)
>
> "No one can come to me unless the Father who sent me draws them, and I will raise them up at the last day.

Often lacking direct experience of God, and sufficient meditation on the Word of God, Christians in the present-age often have their house built on sand, their roots not firmly in the soil, and develop interest in conforming to the patterns of this world, where they misguidedly yearn for Christianity to be *scientific*, but where science is based on sensation (such as sight), and where Christians consequently do not fully grasp that they are to walk by faith, *not by sight*.[41]

---

[41] I am not suggesting that Christians cease doing apologetics, but rather, I am suggesting that they:
- Restrict apologetics to exposing the holes in atheist attackers' blitzes on Christianity and the Bible
- Not get too wound-up trying to *prove* God exists scientifically or logically, which is impossible, since God is known by faith, not by sensation or reasoning
- Keep perspective that the Bible is concerned with *faith* (evidence in the unseen), not with its opposite, which is *science* (evidence of the seen)

One revelation of faith-experience and direct experience of God is more powerful than all apologetics information combined. Atheists are usually not swayed by apologetics, but revelation of Christ can sway for those who are open to Truth.

Atheists are typically concerned with three things:

- Purported logical inconsistency of the Bible
- Hypocritical conduct of Christians
- That there is no scientific or intellectual evidence for God

In this paper, I will discuss how the third point—*that there is no scientific or intellectual evidence for a Christian God*—is absolutely correct, is 100 percent in agreement with the Bible, and since atheists are not in disagreement with the Bible on that point, then claiming that lack of scientific or intellectual evidence for God is problematical for the Bible and Christianity is a red herring, and also a strawman analysis. This is an important point, and atheists have missed the logical contradiction in their analysis of, and attack on, Christianity[42]. Regarding this issue, consider the following points:

1. Atheists claim scientific and intellectual evidence is required to know that the God of the Bible is real.

2. But the God of the Bible is specifically defined in terms of being knowable only by faith-experience, and the Bible specifically says He is *not* known by scientific and intellectual evidence ("we walk by faith, not by sight").

3. Atheists are *not* discussing the God of the Bible according to how it is defined (known by faith, Phil 3:8-9, Heb. 11:6, and other verses quoted in this chapter).

4. This erroneous analysis atheists invent is used to tear down Christianity.

---

[42] To be fair, much of why atheists have made this error is because they are following what many Christians say "faith" is, but where what Christians are saying is not in accord with what the Bible says faith is. This is an incredibly important issue, and it will be explored below.

5. *Therefore*, atheists use strawman analysis in discussing the God of the Bible.

And the specific strawman critical thinking fallacy that atheists routinely carry-out looks like this:

1. The Christian God, by definition, is <u>only</u> knowable by faith-revelation experience ("we walk by faith, not by sight").
2. Atheist claim #1: God <u>must</u> be knowable by scientific and human reasoning processes (which excludes faith-revelation experience).
3. Atheist claim #2: there is no scientific and/or intellectual evidence for the God of the Christian faith.
4. Therefore, the God of the Christian faith should not be believed in, and/or probabilistically speaking almost certainly does not exist. (FALLACY)

This is a textbook critical thinking fallacy, called the strawman, and it exists in virtually every big-name atheists' tool-chest in the contemporary world. Even stranger is that Christians before this chapter of this book have not pointed this obvious critical thinking fallacy out. This is the topic of this chapter.

God is Found Via Faith, Not Via Science or Reason

God is not discoverable in the physical realm, or in the products of human reasoning. This is a critical basic tenet of Christianity, which has not always been overlooked, as it is in the present age. For example, the widely esteemed medieval Byzantine monk and theologian, Maximus the

Confessor, "states that the Godhead has left no traces of itself within creation".[43]

Isaiah 45:15 King James Version (KJV)

15 Verily thou art a God that hidest thyself, O God of Israel, the Saviour.

Scientific work of any sort has no impact on if the God of the Bible exists or not. For example, if the theory of evolution happened to be *correct*, that would not furthermore lead to the conclusion that the Christian God *does not* exist, or that He *does* exist, since one could claim that the Bible is in-line with the theory of evolution, or that is it not in-line with the theory of evolution, but where nobody can be really sure either way. The Christian God could exist regardless of if the theory of evolution were true or not, since the theory of evolution is about matters of science, not matters of faith, and the two theories have nothing to do with each other. The same is true for any scientific position. Whether the Big Bang Theory is true or not likewise does not determine whether or not theism is correct, for example. The same can be said of any scientific position, and any intellectual or logical position of any sort. Science and the Bible are simply in different realms of discourse: Verily thou art a God that hidest thyself.

Many Christians are unaware that the Bible specifically states that *humans will not find evidence for God outside of faith and revelation expe*rience, and they often erroneously believe there is a problem when an atheist or scoffer confronts them saying, "there is no evidence for your Christian God, so I am

---

[43] Bingaman, Brock, 2013, All Things New: The Trinitarian Nature of the Human Calling in Maximus the Confessor and Jürgen Moltman, Princeton Theological Monograph Series, Eugene, OR: Pickwick Publications, p. 18.

most rational to believe it does not exist." Typically, Christians respond saying, "oh no, there *is some scientific or intellectual evidence* for God," and often consequently give awkward, uninformed, and even absurd opinions in a desperate attempt to show there *is* scientific or intellectual evidence for God, other than faith-revelation. But the proper response the Christian should have given is this,

> "Correct, *the only way to know God is through the revelation of faith experience*, which is not scientific or intellectual in any way, we therefore expect science, logic, and mathematics *not* to discover God,"

wherein the Christian can then move-on to the next topic (such as discussing the breakthrough-joy of supernatural faith experience).

Atheism Reduces to Contradiction

Speaking for a moment just about science (empirical investigation), it is self-evidently true that it simply makes no sense, and perhaps is even contradictory, to try to discover a non-empirical (and supernatural) entity through empirical means.

And likewise, one cannot utilize empirical means in attempting to claim either that

- There is a lack of empirical evidence for a non-empirical entity
- The lack of empirical evidence shows the non-empirical entity does not exist

These claims would each reduce to contradiction. The top bullet point is used by more sophisticated atheists, in order to avoid an informal fallacy of ignorance, but the statement still appears to involve contradiction, since it is a means of trying to discuss and discover the _non-empirical_ only in terms of the _empirical_, which is like trying to discover and discuss the non-mathematical, and that which _cannot_ be mathematical, by using _only_ using mathematics. And the second/bottom bullet point is used by more uncouth atheists, who are not aware that the bottom bullet involves the informal fallacy of ignorance, in addition to the aforementioned contradiction of analyzing the purely non-empirical by solely empirical means.

But these methods appear to be, nevertheless, a standard means of investigation among atheists, when atheists attempt to utilize science in showing that God does not exist, or that there is no evidence for God.

Revelation and Non-revelation Evidence

As stated in the introduction, the claim of this paper is that much of the atheism-theism debate that has existed for a long time is about an imaginary / not-real issue, and that imaginary issue is this: _whether or not there is, or is not, scientific and/or intellectual evidence for existence of the Christian God._ (Hereafter I will only refer to the _Christian_ God, the God of the Bible, in what follows.) This topic is essentially like debating how many unicorns exist, or like debating how many people live on Mars.

Stating this issue in better detail, consider the following two points:

A. Atheism involves the position that there is a lack of scientific, logical, or mathematical evidence needed to confidently believe in a Christian God.

B. The Bible *also* clearly indicates that there is no scientific, logical, or mathematical evidence available that will show any person that they should believe in the Christian God.[44]

A and B perfectly agree, since as many Christians know, "we walk by faith not by sight," which atheists would be unaware of since they have no capacity to know that faith experience is real.

The salvific Christian knows God not by science and human-based information, but rather by *being pulled to God directly* (John 6:44), and by being chosen by God (John 15:16)—*not* by trying to understand Him according to human ways of understanding (science and reason). God is infinite (Psalm 147:5 KJV) and God is Mystery that is not fully knowable (Col. 2:2-4, Eph. 3), so human-based ways of understanding God fall into heresy—such as by claiming that God is knowable by science (which includes and is dominated by *sight* information), but where we are told in the Word that:

> 2 Corinthians 5:6-7 New International Version (NIV)
>
> 6 Therefore we are always confident and know that as long as we are at home in the body we are away from the Lord. 7 For we live by faith, not by sight.

In this chapter, I will consider evidence in terms of four categories:

---

[44] As introduced above, the Bible only points to experiential, first person, evidence for God (faith), which is, by definition, is not scientific, logical, or mathematical.

1. *Scientific evidence*: information of the senses (physical evidence). There is zero evidence of this sort for the existence of the Christian God.[45]

2. *Logical evidence*: intellectual information to do with human reason and systems of logic. This category would include mathematics, philosophical logic, conceptual arguments, and so on. There is zero evidence of this sort for the existence of the Christian God.

3. *Ontological evidence*: information about reality that does not fit into 1 and 2: time, minds and mental content, causation, space, etc. The information in this category that coincides with 1 or 2 above would not serve as evidence for a God of the Bible, but any evidence in this category that coincides with 4 below could serve as *personal* (first-person) evidence for the existence of the Christian God, depending on the circumstances (such as that the first-person experience is not mere hallucination, for example).

4. *Supernatural experiential evidence (faith-revelation)*: information about reality that is *experiential* supernatural content experienced by one mind/consciousness, or perhaps experienced by a small collection of minds/consciousnesses. This information is not of categories 1 and 2 above, and may or may not be of category 3 above. Examples of supernatural experiential evidence (faith-revelation) could be: a powerful conversion experience, a vision of the Christian God, or a

---

[45] To my knowledge, many Christians, perplexingly, believe that Romans 1:20 indicates that humans are expected to witness, or see, the evidence of God *in nature*. But as I discussed in Chapter 2, Romans 1:20 specifically says nothing even remotely close to that. God making Himself known to people can occur in many ways other than through "nature revelation," if there is such a thing, such as via confirmations and signs, visions, miracles, answered prayer, and the list is large. In fact, also as discussed in Chapter 2 above, Romans 1:20 even makes it clear that vision is apparently not being what is referred to in that verse, since that verse refers to God's "invisible qualities" (NIV) and thus this would indicate that Romans 1:20 is not about vision experience and so-called (and somewhat pagan-sounding) "nature revelation."

moment of faith during prayer to Christ, wherein a person experiences the supernatural spiritual realm, where one is in bodily form on earth, but in mind and spirit may not be fully in the physical dimension: "Therefore we are always confident and know that as long as we are at home in the body we are away from the Lord." It is here and only here that one can have evidence for the existence of the God of the Bible, and therefore, evidence for God is never scientific or intellectual, and evidence for the Christian God will only be found in personal faith-based revelation. The Bible is very specific on these matters: *we talk by faith, not by sight.*

Let's narrow the categories of evidence just given into two camps:

i.   *Non-revelation evidence*, and

ii.   Evidence in 4, *faith-revelation evidence/experience.*

ii gives evidence of the God of the bible, i does not.

If I have missed any evidence of any sort (such as dream information, or parapsychological information, if any exists, and so on) that others believe should be included in the evidence list, or if some disagree with how the list is arranged above, I confidently believe that changes to the above evidence categories could be made rather freely and still fit into either i or ii. That is my only concern: that there is a demarcation between (ii) supernatural revelation evidence/experience ("faith is... evidence of the unseen," Heb. 11:1 KJV), and (i) non-revelation evidence and/or experience. Restating these categories of evidence once more, in different words:

i.   *Non-revelation information and evidence* does not involve information about a supernatural reality, and

ii.   *Revelation information and evidence* does involve direct (perhaps even non-representational) information about a supernatural reality ("faith-based revelation").

The Bible does *not* contain any statements that say anything like this:

a. In the Last Days (between Christ's ascension and Eschaton) you will have the ability to experience God with your senses, such as with your sense of sight.[46]

b. You can successfully develop mathematical and/or intellectual sure-thing proofs for the existence of God.

c. The ontology and scientific theories developed by men can "reach into" Heaven and show with certainty that God exists.

The Bible says none of this—nothing even comparable. It arguably claims the opposite, and it only claims that humans can have *experiential* evidence for Him: first person revelation experience/evidence for the existence of God, which is not 1 - 3, nor anything like a – c.

Christianity Involves Fixing Our Eyes On What is Supernatural (God)

As stated above, the Bible and atheism are in complete agreement with how much non-revelation evidence (scientific, logical, mathematical evidence) there is for the existence of the Christian God: precisely *zero*.

---

[46] The Bible, of course, does tell us how there was a time, when Jesus was on earth, wherein humans *could* directly see God with their physical eyes, but that is not the case now, as Paul informed us ("we talk by faith, not by sight"), while we wait for the Second Coming.

This may come as a surprise to many, but that's only due to the dramatic misunderstanding and lack of understanding over what the Bible is saying, and over how sophisticated the Bible is (supernaturally speaking). People, including *many* Christians, humorously typically consider the Bible to be an antiquated book that requires the help of scholars for interpretation and understanding. Humans usually consider *the Bible* to have problems if it appears confusing, rather than *the human mind* as having problems and the Bible being too great to be fully understood by a human. A book written by God can be nothing other than the ultimate engineering textbook of existence, and the ultimate blueprint of Reality. And for those reasons, the Bible discusses an advanced state of being, of seeing, of experiencing, missed by most humans on earth, that is simply a different sort of information, of knowledge, as compared to scientific, logical, and intellectual information (non-revelation evidence). Consider these two points:

I.   Scientific evidence is empirical evidence, that which is obtained by the senses, one of which is *sight*.

II. Consider the well-known verse, 2 Cor. 5:7, which states, "We walk by faith, *not by sight*."

If we combine I and II, we can formulate the following informative point:

III. The scientific / empirical sort of non-revelation evidence depends on vision with the physical eyes (sight), Christian faith specifically *does not* depend on vision with the physical eyes (sight), (or any sensation), and therefore, *science cannot discover, discuss, or include the Christian God as a referent, and Christian faith* is in a different universe of discourse than any scientific / empirical analysis can involve.

Non-revelation experience on the one hand, and the God of the Bible on the other, are separated, alienated by a non-intersecting divide. So it is mysterious as to why atheists and theists are endlessly debating the existence of the Christian God in terms of science and the non-revelation forms of evidence. The Bible on the one hand, and the intellectual pursuits of science and logic on the other, are simply not talking about the same aspects of reality: they are not on the same side of the street, so to speak. Science is focused on physical reality via the senses, and the Bible is focused on the opposite: on supernatural reality *not through the senses*. Consider the following Scriptural evidence:

Colossians 3:1 King James Version (KJV)

If ye then be risen with Christ, seek those things which are above, where Christ sitteth on the right hand of God.

Philippians 3:20 New International Version (NIV)

But our citizenship is in heaven. And we eagerly await a Savior from there, the Lord Jesus Christ,

Hebrews 3:1 New International Version (NIV)

Therefore, holy brothers and sisters, who share in the heavenly calling, fix your thoughts on Jesus, whom we acknowledge as our apostle and high priest.

Psalm 123:2 New International Version (NIV)

As the eyes of slaves look to the hand of their master, as the eyes of a female slave look to the hand of her mistress, *so our eyes look to the Lord* our God till he shows us his mercy [Itals added].

Romans 12:12 English Standard Version (ESV)

> 12 Rejoice in hope, be patient in tribulation, be <u>constant</u> in prayer.

Look at the last verse (and there are many like this filling the pages of the Bible), which tells us to be *ceaselessly* focused on Christ: ceaselessly focused on the *supernatural*, not the natural/scientific. Ceaseless awareness of God is one of the dominant themes of the Bible, a message seemingly found in one form or another on most pages of the Bible. In its most pure form, Christianity is an around-the-clock communion with, and meditation on, the indwelling Logos. But that leads to an important question:

> *How can one find God through sense information if the Bible is instructing humans to, specifically, not to find Him through the senses, but to find Him via supernatural faith-revelation?*

Answer: one cannot, and God is not found via sensation, He is found by faith. God, in His omnipresence, coincides with this world, but He is not part of this world: He is *in all things* (Eph. 4:6, 4:10, Isa 6:3) but not of the world. Christian faith is about direct, inner[47] connection to God (faith), believing in God, and therefore about *experience* of God:

> Hebrews 11:1 King James Version (KJV)
>
> Now faith is the substance of things hoped for, the <u>evidence</u> of things not seen.

The Bible specifically tells us not to focus on the works of humans, such as non-revelation evidence (science, human intellectualism), but to focus

---

[47] Ephesians 3:16 New International Version (NIV): "I pray that out of his glorious riches he may strengthen you with power through his Spirit in your inner being…"

beyond that, to the supernatural via the connection, the channel, to God who is everywhere, which is called _faith_:

> 1 Corinthians 2:5 English Standard Version (ESV)

> 5 so that your faith might not rest in the wisdom of men but in the power of God.

Faith is Nonscientific / Trans-Scientific Experience of the Supernatural

Notice that in the King James Bible, Hebrews 11:1 indicates that faith is a type of _evidence_. Faith is merely evidence of a Reality not available to non-revelation types of evidence. In simpler terms, faith involves awareness and experience of the supernatural realms, unseen by the physical eyes (but not unseen by the spiritual eyes and the eyes of the mind), and transcendent of known logic and human reasoning—but experienceable nevertheless by the inner mind and heart of the human, where human language, logic, and science cannot articulate or fathom.

Faith involves human energy, but the connection, the relationship of faith, is an instrument, a gift, _from God, coming from Heaven_, not from the world (culture or nature):

> Hebrews 12:2 New International Version (NIV)

> 2 fixing our eyes on Jesus, the pioneer and perfecter of faith. For the joy set before him he endured the cross, scorning its shame, and sat down at the right hand of the throne of God.

Note how this verse ties together "fixing our eyes on Jesus" with Him being the author of faith. This gives us a hint as to what faith actually is—which is an awareness of, and connection to, God. This is important, because below we will briefly explore what the Bible actually says faith is, and we will conclude that billions of people on earth are not paying enough attention to the specifics of what the Bible says faith is, and therefore they are confused about what this all-important Christian concept involves.

Notice that II and III, above indicate that Christian faith, which is the instrument of one's relationship with, and connection to, the Christian God, is non-scientific, for the following reasons:

> God is telling humans through 2 Cor. 5:7 that faith (in Christ) is to be sought *without* sensation (such as sight), and thus specifically *not* with science, wherein information through the eyes (and senses) is therein literally not a trusted source of information, with respect to knowing *ultimate knowledge.*

Consider Galatians 5:25:

> Galatians 5:25 King James Version (KJV)

> 25 If we live in the Spirit, let us also walk in the Spirit.

The NIV says "let us keep in step *with the Spirit.*" Again, we are told to walk not by what is scientific/empirical, but rather by what is specifically *not* scientific: *Spirit* (i.e., God).

The Bible is telling people of earth that if they want to know God, not to pointlessly try to find him with sensation (science) or with theories and reasoning that is far from being 100 percent certain, but *rather* to find Him directly, with their minds, their spiritual eyes, and their hearts:

> Psalm 105:4 New American Standard Bible (NASB)

> 4 Seek the Lord and His strength; Seek His face continually.

The claim of this verse is strong: seek God (who is not scientifically/empirically discoverable) always, and comparably the information of the senses is not of importance:

> 2 Corinthians 4:18 New International Version (NIV)

> 18 So we fix our eyes not on what is seen, but on what is unseen, since what is seen is temporary, but what is unseen is eternal.

> Matthew 18:9 King James Version (KJV)

> 9 And if thine eye offend thee, pluck it out, and cast it from thee: it is better for thee to enter into life with one eye, rather than having two eyes to be cast into hell fire.

The Biblical Definition of Faith (Is Not the One that People Use)

There is a great rift between what atheists and contemporary Christians claim faith is during their atheist-theist debates, on the one hand, and what the Bible specifically says faith is, on the other. So, what I am saying is that _both_ Christians and atheists are making an error of not defining faith in terms of what the Bible says it is. There is what atheists and Christians claim faith is, on the one hand, and then there is what the Bible says it in fact is on the other (the Bible says it is experience-evidence, but not scientific evidence and logical reasoning known to humans: non-revelation evidence). Consider the erroneous way faith is defined versus the Bible's way:

> _Popular non-Biblical definition of "faith"_ used in atheism versus theism debates, ubiquitously used by atheists:

"Belief without evidence" (this is from Peter Boghossian).[48]

Since the Bible says faith is a type of *evidence* (Heb. 11:1 KJV, NLT, etc.), this description of faith used by atheists is a strawman.

Christians commonly, popularly, and loosely, toss around the following incomplete definitions of "faith" (it is partial, and therefore not fully Biblical, as to what "faith" actually denotes):

"Trust in God" (common Christian usage of definition of faith).

"Believe in God" (common Christian usage of definition of faith).

Then there is the *Biblical definition of "faith"* according to the Bible verses given in this chapter that specifically use the word "faith" in them:

Faith is being directly connected to, fully aware of, directly experiencing God, at all times,[49] and by that, in a state of constant (ceaseless) *believing* (present-tense) in, and communion with, Trinity at all times.[50]

---

[48] Peter Boghossian, the author of *A Manual For Creating* Atheists (Pitchstone 2013), says this in a debate with Dr. Tim McGrew, Sept. 24, 2014, https://www.premierchristianradio.com/Shows/Saturday/Unbelievable/Episodes/Peter-Boghossian-vs-Tim-McGrew-A-manual-for-creating-atheists. Boghossian says in this interview that billions of Christians use the definition of faith in this way, and I would agree with him on this. Unfortunately Boghossians view, while it agrees with billions of contemporary Christians, it is in stark disagreement with the Bible, such as Heb. 11:1 (especially the KJV translation: "faith is the *evidence* of things unseen"). Of course this is not the only thing discussed about faith in common parlance, and faith is also commonly described as total trust in God, as Tim McGrew says in this same debate with Beghossian, which is, of course, Biblically correct, but this is a point rarely discussed by atheists, who greatly emphasize faith just as Beghossian does here. What Beghossian means is faith is experience without non-revelation evidence, but his definition is not complete, since the Bible is utterly packed with those who had experiential evidence (revelation evidence) of God, such as Damascus Road, and so on. For some strange reason, Christians utterly ignore other dimensions and more prominent Scripture about faith, that describe it in the way we have described theurgical evidence above.
[49] Romans 14:23 says, that which is not of faith is sin.
[50] I will discuss, in Part 3, the daily-life practice of having this most direct way to faith-experience Christ—a state of being I call *God-faith*.

Call the first definition the _popular non-Biblical definition of faith_, and call the last definition the _Biblical definition of faith_. The Biblical definition of faith above comes from only the passages in the Bible that have been given in this chapter, and which specifically have the word "faith" in them. Others define faith in terms of verses that don't use the word "faith", and use other words they believe are synonymous, such as "believe". I will however find this problematical below, and I will derive the definition of faith only from verses that are translated to use the word "faith" in them.

If one merely combines the verses given in this chapter, one will immediately see they will arrive at something like the Biblical definition of faith just given above. I realize that the Biblical definition of faith just given is a little different than most Christians were expecting, but that would be more of a product of

- Christians being unfamiliar with how the Bible defines "faith"
- The fact that Christians erroneously reduce faith down to mere truth and belief, and therein violate what the Bible says faith specifically is.

I have no explanation for why theologians and Christians on the one hand, and atheists on the other, _both_ so relentlessly mis-define and misunderstand "faith", not merely taking the time to simply get the definition from the Bible.

The Bible specifically says that in the End Times that humans will forget God and not be interested in correct doctrine, and the distortion of what the Bible says faith is, that I am discussing in this section, and the next two sections, is, I believe, evidence for this End Times weakening of Christians worldwide.

Faith is Not Reducible to Belief

But what *is* faith? How often is this really explored, in terms of deep analysis of the verses in the Bible that mention the word "faith"?

Belief is a subset of faith, not identical to faith. And by straying from using passages in the Bible that stick to the word "faith" in them to derive our definition of Biblical faith, human interpretation (which the Bible says are lies, Ps. 116:11, Rom. 3:4) creeps in. Consider the (rather inarticulate and verbose) definition of "faith" that John Piper gives in a YouTube video he put out, that is apparently the definition of "faith" Piper used in his book *Future Grace*, which from what I can tell, if one can decipher what Piper is in fact saying in the first place, strays *heavily* from the simple and straightforward Biblical definition of faith just given above.

> Piper writes:
>
> > Faith is being satisfied with all that God is for us in Jesus, not just an assent to truths (past or future) but heartfelt valuing and treasuring of all that God promises to be for us in Jesus.[51]

Bringing up Piper's human-based (non-Biblical) purported definition of faith brings us to an extremely important point:

> *Faith is not just reducible to belief*, since the Bible says faith is a type of evidence, and thus is greater than mere belief, since one can believe without having evidence. Thus, making faith equal to belief would not be in accord with the Biblical definition of "faith".

---

[51] YouTube video, May 22, 2013, "John Piper - Faith defined," YouTube Channel: Desiring God, https://www.youtube.com/watch?v=8tlUw9CrjlM.

Piper makes the move, in his video, to focus on faith as being a synonym with the word "believe." This move is utterly ubiquitous with Christians worldwide, it is utterly erroneous, and it is where, for example, Beghossian gets his definition of "faith." In other words, Beghossian gets his definition of faith *not* from the Bible, but from Christians (who are not aware of what the Bible specifically says faith *is*). It is so ubiquitous that Christians (and atheists) define "faith" as being "belief" and no more than that, that Piper does not even bother to point out that he's equating the two—he just makes the move as if everyone listening already "knows" that faith=belief. But we just pointed out that belief and faith *are not equal*, since belief is a subset of faith, and the one is greater than the other.

If faith = belief, then why in the Bible is there a need for two words, both "faith" and "belief", why the extra word "faith"? Why not just always use "believe"? The answer is because faith is more specific than "believe," and greater than the rarely defined, and hard-to-define, concept of simple human belief.

Given the verses we've explored in this chapter that refer to "faith", there is no way possible we can merely define "faith" as merely being *belief*—to say that faith is just a type of belief. Now when Piper, for example, makes this move, three things happen:

- What the Bible says faith is, becomes distorted
- Verses in the Bible that *do not* refer to faith, but instead, for example, refer to *belief*, are used as if they are giving a full definition of "faith"
- Verses in the Bible that do not reference faith, but only reference belief, are believed to be about faith, and used to defined "faith". In other words, Acts 16:30-31 may be believed to be verses that define what

faith is, and therefore verses that don't even include the word "faith" are used to define *what faith is.*

And the result is that by making the move to consider faith as mere belief, and where "belief" remains largely undefined, the message about what faith is, from the Bible, becomes completely distorted at best, and totally lost at worst. In other words, the all-important concept of faith becomes lost in Piper's words ("the words of men"), as the Biblical definition, which is totally different than Piper's definition, is completely unknown in Piper's influential work.

The true definition, merely taken from the Bible, is that faith means *evidence* of the unseen (Heb. 11:1), not just believing in the unseen, which can happen without evidence, just as I can believe in Santa Claus without evidence. But Christian faith is believing *with* (supernatural) *evidence, which is revelation experience.* The importance of this point cannot be underestimated, and this is the number one confusion, in my opinion, that exists among Christians in the world today. Faith is being *aware of Christ*, because we fix our eyes on Him (Heb. 12:2)—that is far more than mere "belief without evidence."

Atheists typically define faith as Piper does, as a synonym for believe, which is not in-line with the Bible, and allows one to fall into the popular *non-Biblical* definition of faith that Boghossian elaborated on above, believing without evidence, which is standard for Christians to do (as it is *also* for atheists) and since so many Christians purport that God exists but don' have any faith-experience (revelation, evidence of the unseen). The NLT translation also uses the word "evidence" to define faith in Hebrews 11:1, and other translations use "certainty," "conviction," or "assurance" of things unseen. The HCSB uses "proof". And look at the AMP:

Hebrews 11:1 Amplified Bible (AMP)

11 Now faith is the assurance (title deed, confirmation) of things hoped for (divinely guaranteed), and the evidence of things not seen [the conviction of their reality—faith comprehends as fact what cannot be experienced by the physical senses].

(That is precisely now the AMP reads, I have not inserted any changes.)

Atheists seemingly continually believe that 2 Cor. 5:7 means something like what Boghossian says, when he says that the popular non-Biblical definition of "faith" is, *believing without evidence.* This error in understanding the definition of "faith" is an error Christians also make almost as ubiquitously as atheists do, and the error stems from failing to understand that faith is a type of supernatural *experience, of "something,"* not a mere worldview data-point that is without referent (such as believing in Santa Claus). We know this not only due to the quoted verses that refer to faith and use the word "faith" that have been given in this chapter, but also because the Bible is littered with examples of supernatural revelation experience as the tool God uses to make Himself known. Atheists usually claim that faith is merely a baseless choice Christians have made, with no substance behind it (Christians *very* often use this same definition), in order to comfortably believe there is a God rather than face the abyss of nothingness in not believing in a God.

Faith is Revelation Experience

The most important point is that, sadly,

Most Christians, in today's world, do not understand that the Biblical definition of faith <u>must</u> involve constant experience of God (revelation), if it did not, then the Bible would not say "in your presence there is fullness of joy" (Ps. 16:11), "pray without ceasing (1 Thess. 5:17), seek His face continually (Ps. 105:4 NIV), and the basis of knowing God is via faith (Phil. 3:8-9).

This one missed point—*the Biblical definition of faith*—leads to unfathomable confusion and misguidedness about Christianity worldwide!

The Bible is talking about Christianity as an experiential conviction, and not as an intellectual decision: as a life of communion and revelation in Christ, not a worldview position. The visions, revelations, God-presence, etc., that glut the Bible, and which *precede* people dedicating their lives to Christ (e.g., Damascus Road, etc.), show that faith must involve experience of God ("*evidence* of the unseen"), not a choice to include Him in our worldview.

Faith is a *different* sort of information, of evidence, than science, logic, and reason, a *different* sort of information than atheists can fathom, than they have available to them, and given their lack of experience of faith, they appear to have merely misinterpreted what faith is described as in the Bible. And if they deny what I just said, they may fall into the fallacy of ignorance, which would go as follows:

1. By definition, Christian faith-revelation-experience evidence would be evidence *not available* to atheists.
2. The atheist claims they have no evidence to believe this "different sort of information, of evidence," called that faith-revelation exists,
3. *Therefore*, faith-revelation-experience evidence does not exist (FALLACY).

That is a textbook fallacy of ignorance informal critical thinking fallacy, that would be just like this one: I have never seen your mind, I have no evidence that your mind exists, therefore, your mind does not exist.

Miracles

In Christianity, miracles present a special case for understanding how important faith is to Christianity.

The four Gospels and the writings of Paul show us two things:

- The Christian should be experiencing miracles regularly in their Christian life
- For those without the non-empirical evidence of faith-revelation experience, miracles will not be observable (regardless if the person is an atheist to a churchgoer)

Consider the following situation. I pray with two men, man1 and man2, according to the following setup:

- Man1 has faith-revelation (he is salvific), and man2 is faithless (he is perishing)
- One of the men has a seriously sick father, and asks me to pray for immediate healing
- I pray, the presence of God is lived and experienced during the prayer, and thus that faith-experience drives the prayer
- An hour after I leave, a phone-call is received by the man with the sick father that the father is undergoing an inexplicable, shocking improvement

- Man1 witnesses the miracle and his inner-being is deeply affected
- Man2 does not see a miracle and his inner-being is unmoved by the event

It will not be possible for man2 to understand situation or the connection. And this will be true no matter how many times this sort of scenario takes place. One simply cannot see a miracle of God, even if the Red Sea is parted, or a man with a withered hand healed (Mt. 12), unless one first has faith—unless one's self is fully given to God, so it can fully reside in its true state of existence: *in Christ*. Without faith—without belief in God, to the point of directly experiencing Him—the presence of God cannot exist in a person and their faith cannot heal, and their eyes cannot see.

Jeremiah 5:21 New King James Version (NKJV)

21 'Hear this now, O foolish people,

Without understanding,

Who have eyes and see not,

And who have ears and hear not...

Matthew 13:15 New King James Version (NKJV)

15 For the hearts of this people have grown dull.

Their ears are hard of hearing,

And their eyes they have closed,

Lest they should see with their eyes and hear with their ears,

Lest they should understand with their hearts and turn,

So that I should heal them.'

For the purposes of this book, we can use the simple definition of miracles that philosophers often use: a miracle is a violation or interruption of the laws of nature. As others before me have also noted, that to be a Biblically-oriented miracle has to be ascribed to God, caused by Him and leading to revelation of God: _God is the supernatural cause of the interrupting and violating of nature._

So, then, the faithless (such as man2, or such as some of the Pharisees in Matthew 12, whose hearts were hardened by witnessing Jesus's miracles) can witness miracles, but outside of faith, they do not experience them as miracles, and only experience their selfish, fear-filled, and desire-filed nature, which blinds the mind, and blocks revelation of God. If one doubts how much desires, fears, and selfishness blocks awareness of reality, all one has to do is think if an extreme situation in their life, such as a situation of fear, and how afterwards one thought, "wow, I can't believe how unclearly I was thinking." Note how much the fear in fact distorted awareness of reality, and then note how often this happens at lower levels in a person's life, and therefore how pervasively this sort of blinding to reality life involves. Truth is hidden from a person unless perfect love casts out all fear, and unless desire and selfishness are crucified with Christ. A person not fully surrendered to Christ cannot see, and is blinded to the miracles of Christ going on all around, intervening in nature.

Man1 and man2 can both witness the same arrangements of atoms in physical reality, but only one will see _past_ physical reality, to have direct revelation of the Source of the atomic arrangements, and by faith-revelation experience God's power in the miracle.

For these reasons, a miracle can only be defined as what we can call a *Christological miracle*, since any miracle that is caused by the Christian God can simultaneously only be a miracle where God is *known* through it, and in it, and, *ipso facto*, is a faith experience. So, we can define a Christological miracle as:

> *Christological miracle*: A perceived interruption and violation in the physical stream of events in nature that contains the awareness that the Christian God is the cause and source for the interruption and violation, and where the specific point of the interruption is to directly reveal God to human consciousness (faith-revelation experience).

This is the Biblical view of a miracle, and it only provides evidence for the existence of God via faith-evidence. That is why, in the Bible, some could see a miracle, and others could not, while looking at the same physical events, the same arrangements of atoms in physical reality, such as in how some Pharisees were aware of the miracle in the raising of Lazarus from the dead, but while others were only filled with anger and hatred over this event. For this reason, a miracle of God can never be scientific, as that would violate the definition of what faith is. Hence, God hides himself, is not revealed in nature, and when breaking through into physical reality to show Himself by disrupting physics, the disruptions only are seen via faith (and the disruptions are seen regularly by those of ceaseless faith). And likewise, the truth of who the Christian God is, and His realness, could never be known through intellectual accounts either. For example, if a person formulated the perfect argument that proved God existed beyond a shadow of a doubt, with the simplest of logic, it would function like a miracle, since it will contain revelation of God—but the argumentation could only be recognized if faith was in place in the observer of the argumentation.

Conclusion

It is perhaps mysterious as to why the points of this chapter have been missed by so many on both sides of the theism-atheism debate. That Christians and atheists, past and present, wound-up in atheism vs. theism issues, have not noticed that the Bible and atheism are in agreement on the fact that science and non-revelation experience do not reveal God, is surprising, and seems to even reveal a mass blindness among men in the world. The Bible is logically coherent in claiming that the there is no non-revelation evidence for God, but atheism reduces to contradiction when and if atheists make this same claim, as discussed in Section 2 above, and as I will be discussing in much more detail in an upcoming article.

But on that note, the Bible does predict such blindness would happen in the Last Days (i.e., after Pentecost, to the present time), where Christians will lose sight (pun intended) of God, and would not carefully follow the supernatural book that was written for us by God (the Bible):

2 Timothy 4:3-4 New International Version (NIV)

3 For the time will come when people will not put up with sound doctrine. Instead, to suit their own desires, they will gather around them a great number of teachers to say what their itching ears want to hear. 4 They will turn their ears away from the truth and turn aside to myths.

6. Murder in the Bible Not Contradict "Thou Shall Not Kill"

Introduction: God Says "No Killing" and then Commands a Lot of Killing to Happen.

In the extremely popular video series, *The Power of Myth* (also made into a book), the famous professor of mythological literature from Sarah Lawrence College, Joseph Campbell voiced the following complaint about an apparent contradiction in the Bible:

> In bounded communities, aggression is projected outward. For example, the ten commandments say, "Thou shalt not kill." Then the next chapter says, "Go into Canaan and kill everybody in it." That is a bounded field. The myths of participation and love pertain only to the in-group, and the out-group is totally *other*.[52]

The Canaanite obliteration is just one of a plethora of utter annihilations God's people carried-out in the Bible. There are killings of all sorts by the people of God in the Bible: war-killings and annihilations, individual killings, killings of children, and so forth. Humans are commanded by God to kill both before and after the Sixth Commandment ("Thou shalt not kill") is laid down as Law in Exodus 20, and throughout the entire Old Testament.

---

[52] This is from the first chapter, "Myth and the Modern World", of *Power of Myth*, by Joseph Campbell and Bill Moyers.

It is widely help by atheists and those who oppose Christianity, that there is quite obvious and glaring contradiction of the Sixth Commandment, since God commands killings, and God's people partake in killings. At first glance, the situation seems to be obvious hypocrisy and contradiction, b, none-other than God Himself, where God says "Thou shall not do X," and then God commands X almost immediately after, and then very regularly throughout the Old Testament, and into the New Testament, where God and God's people can be seen to do X (kill) throughout the Old Testament after "Thou shall not kill" is made law.

And from what I can tell, this is an issue that Christians—from seminary professors to luke-warm Sunday Christians—have no clue how to respond to, completely unaware that the idea that there is a contradiction is based on a misunderstanding and misreading of Scripture (which is the idea that God cannot kill and that the Sixth Commandment refers to God). Many atheists have made careers and gained large audiences out of pointing out this supposed contradiction, but if anyone were to pause and deconstruct the concept that any murder described in the Bible specifically _contradicts_ the Sixth Commandment, it would be quickly discovered that _it is logically impossible to fit any two pieces of text in the Bible to make them contradict regarding this issue of murder in the Bible contradict the Sixth Commandment_. This will be quite effortlessly be shown below, just by using the plainest, simplest reading of Scripture. That is specifically what this paper is about: how it is claimed by atheists that there is a contradiction, but no such contradiction can be found it one tries to go and pinpoint it, and furthermore, the way that the Sixth Commandment has been written (God commanding to humans, without referring to Himself in the Sixth Commandment), can never result in a logical contradiction.

This paper will be a testament to the lack of depth that both the atheist community, and the Christian community (including seminarians) are working at in exploring the text of the Bible.

The Specifics of the (Supposed) Contradiction

The Sixth Commandment appears in Exodus 20:13. After this commandment is given, there are a plethora of murders occurring quite regularly throughout the history of the Old Testament, both in the context of war, and outside of it. These are often killings done for God's work, and often visibly by God's direct command or action, in the cases where they are not human-caused sin. Here is the very well-known example of Sampson killing the Philistines:

> Judges 16:28-30 New King James Version (NKJV)
>
> 28 Then Samson called to the Lord, saying, "O Lord God, remember me, I pray! Strengthen me, I pray, just this once, O God, that I may with one blow take vengeance on the Philistines for my two eyes!" 29 And Samson took hold of the two middle pillars which supported the temple, and he braced himself against them, one on his right and the other on his left. 30 Then Samson said, "Let me die with the Philistines!" And he pushed with all his might, and the temple fell on the lords and all the people who were in it. So the dead that he killed at his death were more than he had killed in his life.

Many believe that what they are seeing here is a simple and obvious contradiction to the Sixth Commandment, which can plainly be stated as follows:

God commanded against murder (~M), God commanded and/or caused murders (M) = ~M ^ M (logical contradiction)

'Thou Shalt Not Kill' is a Command to Humans, not God

The entire problem that has caused atheists and theists alike to imagine that there is a contradiction surrounding the Sixth Commandment and killing in the Bible is easy to identify, and is as follows: God directs the Sixth Commandment to people, not to Himself, so He can kill without contradiction, whereas humans cannot kill. We will see that when this misunderstanding is removed from theology, it is logically impossible for contradiction to exist in any aspects of the text of the Bible between killings in the Bible, and the Sixth Commandment.

Consider the following points:

1. "Thou shalt not kill" is a directive to humans, not God giving a command or rule to Himself. If God exterminates any person or persons, then it is just, and He knows when it needs to happen, according to His plans and purposes in predestinational reality. But a person is foolish, and does not know such things, and thus cannot take such matters into their own hands, and rather, must be worked-through by God when profound things such as killing are to happen.

2. The problem reduces to the question of whose volition causes a killing, God's (not sin), or a humans (willful sin, after the Ten Commandments were laid down)? (But we will see below that in either case, regardless of what volition causes a killing, of the Sixth Commandment does not

include God, no contradiction can ever emerge in the Biblical text surrounding the Sixth Commandment.)

These points will start to resolve this issue, and we can see that concern over there being a contradiction in the Bible regarding killings is based on not seeing what the Bible is actually saying, and failing to look at Scripture for what it actually contains, and the false assumption that God cannot kill and the Sixth Commandment is directed at God (God saying the commandment to Himself) is a startling oversight tha millions of people have not noticed, and this shows how sloppy people (both atheists and theists alike) study the actual Biblical text, and how easily gross misunderstandings that deceive millions can emerge. This is almost certainly the same sort of mindset and carelessness that the Pharisees had when they missed the points of Scripture and did not recognize Jesus for what He was, even though He did miracles right in front of them.[53] Indeed, the same sort of carelessness, that is probably caused by having a hardened heart and the consequent blindness, not being able to see Scripture clearly, is safe to conclude is the cause.

The Sixth Commandment

As stated, the specific problem that has led to millions being deceived into falsely believing there is contradiction in the Bible between the Sixth Commandment and killings throughout the Bible is generated by the error in believing that God was talking *about Himself* in the Sixth Commandment.

---

[53] Strictly speaking, the Gospel of John tells us how many Pharisees were actually being converted to be Christ-followers as a result of Jesus raising Lazarus from the dead. So not all Pharisees were of such hard heartedness that they could not be unblinded.

The oversight, made by many of the famous atheists of the world (e.g., Matt Dillahunty), and not noticed by the timid Christians, is startlingly obvious, and goes as follows:

> God commanded humans not to kill, but God Himself is not commanded _not_ to kill. Thus, God _can_ kill, as well as command humans to kill (just as long as God, not free-willed humans, are the cause). By _God's volition_, either directly killing humans, or by working in and through humans to kill other humans, and not by human volition, is Biblical killing after the Sixth Amendment was lain down, with no contradiction with the Sixth Commandment.

From what I can tell, when I read commentary about the Sixth Commandment given by _both_ atheists and critics of the Bible, but also by theists, _they each_[54] appear to (erroneously) believe that the Sixth Commandment says something roughly like the following:

> "No killing of humans is allowed, by God's decree, neither carried-out by God or by any persons" (call this _6C-not-Scripture_).

So, unsurprisingly, when the many people who believe that the Sixth Commandment says what _6C-not-Scripture_ above contains, they believe a contradiction exists in Scripture, and one can hardly blame any atheists and opponents of Christianity from believing that a contradiction has occurred. And likewise, one can hardly blame Christians for having no clue how to get

---

[54] As I have discussed in the past, including on Aron Ra's atheist radio broadcast, this is common that Christians and atheists will be in heated debates over issues that are simply not in the Bible, and/or which are opposite of what the Bible says, but (wrongly) believing they are debating true Christianity. A great example of this is when Christians and atheist debate about faith, which both hold is merely believe without evidence, which contradicts Hebrews 11:1, which states that faith is evidence (see the KJV, among other translations).

out of this serious dilemma that appears to show that their faith contains a staggeringly obvious and stark logical contradiction.

But as noted above, if we merely look at what the Sixth Commandment in Exodus 20 says, it does not say anything like what *6C-not-Scirpture* is saying. Compare *6C-not-Scripture* to the actual text of the Sixth commandment, which does not contain any commentary about God, but only God stating a command to humans:

"Thou shalt not kill" (call this *6C-Scripture*).

The actual text of Sixth Commandment (*6C-Scripture*) is quite different than saying something like "No killing of humans is allowed, by God's decree, neither carried-out by God or by any persons" (*6C-not-Scripture*). And in some important ways, *6C-not-Scripture* and *6C-Scripture* are *opposites*. Consider the differences between the erroneous way the Sixth Commandment imagined (*6C-not-Scripture*), versus the actual Scripture of the Sixth Commandment (*6C-Scripture*):

"No killing of humans is allowed, carried-out by God or by any persons" (**6C-not-Scripture**)	*"Thou shalt not kill"* (**6C-Scripture**)
Involves the (non-Scriptural) idea that God is forbidden from doing any killing, and involves the non-Scriptural idea that the Sixth Commandment is a command directed at God (He directed it at	Involves God speaking to humans, where humans are given a law, and where it's not the case that God is given a law. So actual Scripture (*6C-Scripture*) *only* says humans are not to do killing, says nothing

Himself), rather than at humans only.	about if God can do any killing or not.
Non-Scripturally forbids God killings, calls them "contradiction."	Permits God killings, and no contradiction follows when God causes killings.

Note that it appears that millions, if not billions, of people on Earth, including atheists, pastors, and professors on both sides of the fence, appear to erroneously believe that *6C-not-Scripture* is what the Sixth Commandment is saying, when it's actually saying very much the opposite.[55]

When I hear atheists discuss the Sixth Commandant, it is always erroneously presented as *6C-not-Scripture*, wherein *6C-not-Scripture* is used in strawman analysis in debating about the supposed contradiction in the Bible surrounding the Sixth commandment. *6C-not-Scripture* involves the incorrect idea that God cannot do any killings, and to debate the Sixth Commandment in terms of *6C-not-Scripture* is like a debate about the nature of purgatory, or a debate over how long a unicorn's horn is (i.e., a debate about something not know to exist).

The Impossibility of Textual, Logical Contradiction of the Sixth Commandment

Here are all the scenarios, the only scenarios that killing can happen in the Bible, given the contexts the Bible is written within:

---

[55] As I have discussed elsewhere, it is common for Christians to ubiquitously believe that the Bible involves a certain concept, C, where the concept is not in the Bible, and in fact, concept ~C pervades the Bible. There are many examples, but one the idea that God created Hell is a great example.

1. God kills a human *using* another human to do the killing (e.g., Golliath killed by David, massacre of the Canaanites in Deuteronomy 20).
2. God kills a human *without using* another human to do the killing (e.g,. the flood,).
3. A human does a killing by their free-will, God has nothing to do with it at all.

1-3 exhaust all possible scenarios. 1 and 2 are not sin, and do not involve any logical contradiction, and 3 does involve sin, and do not involve logical contradiction. At no place in 1-3 is the Sixth Commandment violated. At no place does contradiction emerge. Whether before or after Exodus 20, regardless of what killing occurs in the Bible, all killings will fit into only one of the three scenarios, 1-3.

The only way that a contradiction can emerge surrounding the Sixth Commandment is fully controlled by God but expected to have full free-will. This is an obvious absurdity—but this is what those who claim there is a contradiction surrounding the Sixth Commandment are entailing. In different words, (B) if God commands a killing, it automatically is not a contradiction to the Sixth Commandant, since God is the cause, rather than the human; and (A) if a human, out of his own free-will, kills, amid his residing in the nothingness of sin, it is disobedience to God's law (sin), and not created or caused by God. There are no other options than A and B, and it is impossible that they involve contradiction. Here are all and the only scenarios that the Biblical killings can happen:

The resolution to the apparent contradiction involves humans *who are acted-through, and acted-upon, by God, unfreely* (as slaves of God), wherein they are not the reason the killing happened. And if God is the impetus and cause of a killing, then the humans commanded and controlled by God to help with the killing contribute no sin or contradiction, just as long as humans are not _the cause of_ the killing, and instead _God is_. Some may imagine there is a problem here, since God cannot control free-willed humans. But humans only have free will sporadically, and otherwise we humans are slaves, either to sin and self (Mark 7:15, John 8:34) on the one hand, or we are slaves to Christ (1 Cor. 7:7) on the other.

What I mean by God or a person being the "cause of a killing" is as follows:

> If God were removed from having any interaction in the killing event, then the killing would not have happened, so God is a necessary causal factor in the killing event.

Anything other than this would involve the free-will of humans to kill, as the cause of the killing, and that is what the Sixth Commandment indicates is sin. So, please note that the goal of this paper is very specific: _To show that killing by God and God's people in the Old Testament after the Sixth Commandment is established does contain any logical contradiction._

I imagine many readers will want to side-step the very specific issue I am discussing, and instead focus on how troubling it is that the Bible is replete with killing, and God-endorsed killing, in the first place. That is a very good topic for discussion, but that is specifically _not_ what I am discussing in this short paper.[56] So, to repeat, my only intention is to show the pure logical coherence and noncontradiction of the Bible regarding killings orchestrated by God and by God's people.

---

[56] That issue will be covered in a future paper. Christians do not like to discuss it, but killing something that God does, and killing and/or letting-die is something He is possibly doing at every second, if we agree with the concept than when a person is to die is determined and/or allowed by God

Examples from the Bible

So, it seems plausible to assert that the Sixth Commandment literally intends the following:

> Humans are not allowed to kill of their own free-willed volition, but God can kill as needed, even if using a human (not of their own free volition or choosing) to do so.

Let's go back to the case of Sampson killing the Philistines. Judges 16:28-30 New King James Version (NKJV)

> 28 Then Samson called to the Lord, saying, "O Lord God, remember me, I pray! Strengthen me, I pray, just this once, O God, that I may with one blow take vengeance on the Philistines for my two eyes!" 29 And Samson took hold of the two middle pillars which supported the temple, and he braced himself against them, one on his right and the other on his left. 30 Then Samson said, "Let me die with the Philistines!" And he pushed with all his might, and the temple fell on the lords and all the people who were in it. So the dead that he killed at his death were more than he had killed in his life.

Verse 30 says "he killed," as if Sampson did the killing of his own free will. But verse 28 shows Sampson first calling out to the Lord, in a moment of faith (connection to God), where in saying "strengthen me," Sampson has giving his power over to the Lord, and the Lord now holds the reigns. So the "he' referred to in v.30 when it says "he killed" can only referred to a God-possessed Sampson, not a free-willed autonomous Sampson. In different words, when the weak Sampson says "strengthen me," he is saying only referring to the strength of the Lord, since the Story of Sampson makes it quite clear that his strength is only the strength of God, *not* of Sampson. It is the strength that kills the philistines, and the strength is the Lord. This is an instance of God killing humans, point i above.

And here we see David killing Goliath in Jesus name:

1 Samuel 17:45-50 New King James Version (NKJV)

45 Then David said to the Philistine, "You come to me with a sword, with a spear, and with a javelin. But I come to you in the name of the Lord of hosts, the God of the armies of Israel, whom you have defied. 46 This day the Lord will deliver you into my hand, and I will strike you and take your head from you. And this day I will give the carcasses of the camp of the Philistines to the birds of the air and the wild beasts of the earth, that all the earth may know that there is a God in Israel. 47 Then all this assembly shall know that the Lord does not save with sword and spear; for the battle is the Lord's, and He will give you into our hands." 48 So it was, when the Philistine arose and came and drew near to meet David, that David hurried and ran toward the army to meet the Philistine. 49 Then David put his hand in his bag and took out a stone; and he slung it and struck the Philistine in his forehead, so that the stone sank into his forehead, and he fell on his face to the earth. 50 So David prevailed over the Philistine with a sling and a stone, and struck the Philistine and killed him. But there was no sword in the hand of David.

Mark 7:9-13 New International Version (NIV)

9 And he continued, "You have a fine way of setting aside the commands of God in order to observe[a] your own traditions! 10 For Moses said, 'Honor your father and mother,'[b] and, 'Anyone who curses their father or mother is to be put to death.'[c] 11 But you say that if anyone declares that what might have been used to help their father or mother is Corban (that is, devoted to God)— 12 then you no longer let them do anything for their father or mother. 13 Thus you nullify the word of God by your tradition that you have handed down. And you do many things like that."

God's Volition in Killing, Vs. a Human's Volition in Killing

As I see it, the key points are the following:

A. When a free-willed human, disobeys God and kills another person as a result of their free-will, this is the nothingness of sin. By definition God does not cause this.[57]

B. When a God kills, there is no contradiction.

C. With A, killing happens by humans volition and will, and with B, killing happens by God's volition and will.

D. Only if God caused a person to kill as result of their free will can a contradiction occur with the Sixth Commandment—but God causing free will to do some action X is a contradiction (discussed below).

The volition and will of a free-willed human, and the volition and will of God, either are mostly distinct (in the case of a pre-salvific person), or they are coinherent (inside of each other, see John 15:5), and when they are of the

---

[57] Somebody might object here and state that God creates all things (Rev. 4:11, Col. 1:16-17), so He must cause this sin. But sin is not a thing, it is nothingness (absence, of righteousness), and thus is not counted in the "all *things*" that God creates.

latter intermixture (coinherent), the human will is for the most part, or even completely, eclipsed (see Galatians 2:20, Phil. 2:5, Col. 3:11, etc.). This point, as well as point D above, show that the way the Sixth Commandment is written, *it is impossible to involve contradiction of any sort, under any circumstances.* Atheists imagine that God killing humans is a contradiction to the Sixth Commandment, which is it not, as we've seen above, and if it's not, then no other scenarios exist where humans killing other humans can contradict the Sixth Commandment.

Big Picture

God has predestined reality, put every soul in the body it was to go into in His pre-programmed / predestined reality, where each soul needed to be where it was to carry-out God's exact plan. For this purpose, many of the unchosen were needed to fill various roles, as discussed in Romans 9 and other places in Scripture, and in so many cases, God apparently deems that many of the unchosen are no longer needed on earth, and are removed (killed), after their existence is not needed for God's purposes.[58] So, God can kill, but the instructions are that humans, specifically, cannot kill. They are not trustworthy enough, or knowledgeable enough, to know when killings are to be God's work or not, and thus this operation cannot every be carried out by a human, unless, as Scripture shows, God causes it to happen. If, in the modern world, some crazy person kills somebody and says "God commanded me to do it," such information is to be disregarded, since it cannot be deciphered if these are the words of a human, and only if God

---

[58] For copious discussion on the precise mechanics of predestination and specifically why some are chosen and others are not, see Grupp 2018 and 2019.

made it known to you, or me, that such a killing was part of God's plan, could it be deemed part of God's plan.

However, God directly commanding killing, Old-Testament-style, appears to be more of a phenomenon in the Old Testament dispensation, and not after the dispensational change with the Sermon on the Mount. That is why we do see God killing some in the New Testament, but the commands for God killing by using humans to kill is not found in the New Testament.

It's only a free-willed human act of murder that would be a sin, and there's no contradiction there. And God can do a killing He wanted, no matter how absurd or ghastly in the eyes of a human, and a contradiction does not result. It would only be a contradiction if God said to a human, "by your own free will, without me having anything to do with it, you must be the sole cause of the killing—but not only is that not Biblical, but it also does not make any sense: how can God be the cause of another agent's free will? That's like saying A causes B because A does not cause B. Only free-will can be the cause of free-will. The free-will event can only be caused by the person, not by God, lest it not be free-will.

The whole idea that there is any sort of contradiction in the Old Testament regarding killings after Exodus 20 is a tremendous oversight, and based on the error of believing that the Sixth Commandment involves God talking to Himself, commanding Himself, which is not the case. Apparently, humans have just not understood the simple logic of the Bible regarding the Sixth Commandment, and thus misread it (the wisdom of man is foolishness to God). God is speaking *from* His own volition *to* humans, and it does not involve God saying He's talking to humans and to Himself, but rather it's very clear that it's a *commandment,* given *to humans.* So, the Old Testament contains two types of killings: those by free-willed humans, and those by God who is using humans and humans are not the cause. In either case, no contradiction to the Sixth Commandment exists. Those that are caused by free-willed humans are often declared in the Bible as sin (for example, David and Bathsheba), and those that are caused by God working through humans are in places declared to not be sin and are clearly part of God's plans (such as with David and Goliath) in His predestinational reality.

Conclusion

This issue of where Old Testament killings merely being God's work, not the work of humans, has been overlooked by seminary professors, Bible scholars, amateur Bible experts, and so on, for centuries, but is a startlingly obvious issue from Scripture. This is a lesson on how easy it is for humans to misread Scripture, to overlook the obvious of Scripture, and re-invent Christianity as a new religion, rather than merely follow Scripture. Many Christians are very afraid to follow Scripture literally, because they don't know how to handle problems such as this issue of killings in the Old Testament, and given that there is such a readily simple explanation, this matter should serve as a lesson for how one is mistaken for trusting their own understanding of things, rather than leaning not on their own understanding in trying to interpret Scripture.

We can see that even in the most poignant examples of killing in the Bible, such as killing one's own child, for example, despite how disturbed any person is about this even, it does not involve any logical contradiction.

Why did things change if God does not change? Would mean that things changed in the world as humans progressed in God's plan. God did not change, humans did, in their orientation to God. That's why there are different epochs (dispensations), and why the appearance of the law (not the law itself) must change through time. I realize that Bible critics and atheists may not agree with this position in the Bible, but that is not what is being discussed, and that is understandable, since murder is a difficult issue, and one that we humans naturally have in our conscience as something we should not do, whether atheist or theist. But the Old Testament was a different dispensation, the Law of God working with humans in a way not identical to how it works with humans now/today in the post-Sermon-on-the-Mount dispensation we are now in. The Bible is like a computer program, or an engineering schematic, and it is laying out very specific text, which is typically missed, as the average person—whether atheist or Christian—typically has no idea of the depth and technical sophistication of the Bible, which is, of course, supernatural. Through the centuries theology has become weak and ridiculous among the common churchgoer, leading to a great divide between Scriptural text on the one hand, and the average professing Christian, where the two often have little to do with each other (see Grupp 2019 for more information).

PART 3: Nonphysical Calvinism

Since 1995 I have been working on a very specific type of simulation theory. It was based on several incredibly powerful spiritual experiences I had in November of 1995, in the heart of a time that I was a bitter atheist, and that I was very deeply engaged in around-the-clock, moment-to-moment Soto Zen Buddhist meditation, something I developed an extreme passion for at that time in my life (I was 24-25 years old during these religious experiences, that lasted all through 1995, culminating at a peak in November of 1995). The experience in November of 1995 was surprisingly wonderful, a soft-but-powerful ecstasy of true lovingness overtaking me, where I could literally see something that could be described as a gold light everywhere, like an ultra-intense vibrating sunlight. I had intensely studied Buddhism, and practiced it meticulously, but I was absolutely not prepared for these experiences, especially those in November, as I was utterly overtaken and literally in the absolute, ineffable, unfathomable, omnipresent light. The experiences profoundly changed me, permanently. Many people commented on the stark change in me, in my changing from being a rather foolish, rude, and angry atheist, to a joyant, philosophical spiritual-seeker. I became obsessed with the experiences, which, interestingly, all vanished at the end of November 1995, for reasons I did not discover until years later when I became a Christian. The experiences that culminated in November of 1995 led to a clear picture of reality, where our daily experience of the physical world were revealed to be a more-or-less bland, passionless, meaningless movie-screen in the mind, so to speak—nothing but a movie in the mind, like in the movie *The Matrix*—where it was roughly imaginary, and not based on any actually existing 3D physical reality outside of myself. Humans are mere minds, surrounded by the perfected gold light described above, which is real, and which is utter love and beauty and joy—to try to put it into words is really almost a bad idea since it so diminishes the experience. As I said, I became obsessed with getting these experiences again, but I could not, after 1995, and not until I became a Christian years later. What happened at the end of 1995 is very simple: I was wondering what this omnipresent light *was*, and a sort of realization came into my mind (or was put there), that the light was the Christian God. If you look at an object in your experience, say an apple, if you look at it and say to yourself, "what is that object?", a feeling and knowing (a thought) comes into your mind and awareness, within you, that says, "it's an apple," where you know this to be true and correct in your epistemology. So, when I would look at this omnipresent gold lightning I was experiencing, I would ask myself the same sort of simple inquiry," What is this object?", where just as with the apple example, a feeling and knowing (a thought) would come into my mind and awareness within me, that said, "this is the Christian God," where, just as with the apple, I knew this to be true and correct in my epistemology.

But I was, at that time, a very bitter atheist, hateful of Christianity, and I would literally say, in my thoughts and feelings, "No, there is no Christian God, that religion makes no sense, this realization in my mind, this conclusion, that this omnipresent ecstatic gold energetic "sunlight" is the Christian God, has to be a mistake." This inner debate went on for a few days at the end of this entire time in my life in 1995, until I made up my mind, with a definitive, "NO! This is not the light of Christ!" It was around this time that the experiences completely vanished, and I fell into a serious depression, that lasted about five years, and was plagued by what I would no clearly call demonic attacks and activity.

I remained completely obsessed with this experience, and began to read philosophy, research, and try to come to sense of what happened—all while, however, I'd uncontrollably become a rather depressed and dark person, which distracted me until I entered the graduate program in philosophy at Western Michigan University in 2001. There I searched for the specific philosophy, or philosophical theory that most perfectly described what I'd experienced, where I would do my MA thesis research on this field (and later while studying for a PhD at Purdue I roughly continued the same trajectory during the time I was at Purdue). I discovered (or, as I now believe, I was _led to_) a philosophy called mereological nihilism, which was the idea that all that exists are energy points or nonphysical-like atoms, which are all identical to each other, so that it formed a sort of uniform or unchangin8g light or energy that was omnipresent, and our experiences of a physical reality are just a misperception of atomic reality. In other words, reality is a field of unstructured energy, my experiences of physical reality were largely just a picture screen in the mind, much like a computer simulation, like in the movie _The Matrix_.

I immediately recognized that this was obviously the theory I needed to work with, because with a few logical corrections and metaphysical updates, the theory perfectly matched what I'd seen, I believed. All of my initial publications in professional philosophical research were about trying to set up the basis for what was going to be a rock-solid logical philosophy to perfectly describe our reality, which I started to call *abstract atomism*, denoting the nonphysicality of the field of ecstatic reality all around, providing a new description of reality, based on what I'd experienced in November 1995. I was amazed how these publications set up the groundwork for the ecstatic philosophical model of mereological nihilism I was building, until I published a first draft of the full theory, in the professional journal, *Axiomathes*, in 2006.[59] I was still a devout atheist at this time, and I had not yet admitted that the omnipresent light was the light coming off the face of the omnipresent Logos (Jesus Christ). This research in mereological nihilism is what broke my being an atheist, because mereological nihilism led to the conclusion that the mind could not be explained by the field of quantum atomism, and where the mind was distinct from the omnipresent ecstatic energy/light that I'd experienced in 1995, and to put it most simply for our purposes here, the only real explanation for the mind left was that the mind was a sort of nonphysical apparatus made of an unknown medium or structure.

In 2006, mostly because of this situation in publishing my "mereological nihilism" paper, I started to believe in God—not the Christian God at all, but rather some sort of a generic concept of a creator-God that was an ecstatic light that was all around, supernaturally creating nonphysical minds to exist as self-aware computer simulations, generating an artificial experience of a physical world of contradictory physical objects (an experience of a 3D physical world that seemed to be real and outside of oneself all around, but which was actually a sort of movie in the mind, and on more than thjat. This

---

[59] "Mereological Nihilism: Quantum Atomism and the Impossibility of Material Constitution," *Axiomathes: An International Journal in Ontology and Cognitive Systems*, Vol. 16, No. 3, 2006, pp. 245-386.

led to my presentation of a talk at the winter colloquia at the University of Michigan – Dearborn, where I was teaching at the time, on "simulation theory"[60], April of 2013, where I was convinced (and still am), that I presented the first ironclad logical simulation theory. This research has developed through the years, and now some of which is chapter 10 of this book.

It was, however, very shortly after this that I had a rather violent conversion to Christianity (pun intended: the conversion surrounded several visions that culminated in major a car-crash my wife and children were in). And it was some time after that, that I realized that my publication on mereological nihilism was in fact was a model of Christianity, not some other system of thought.

After being a Christian for some time, I became quite preoccupied—and still am up to this instant—with what I now call "omnipresence prayer" (see Chapter 10). I gave a sermon about this on March 17, 2019[61], while I was writing this book. The basic idea is to look out at reality, and _know_, with perfected believing, that God-Logos is the creator of all the matter-forms that I see, that He is distinct from them, but also that He is in all points in my vision-field. This prayerfulness often leads to a similar realization as the November 1995 experience.

I have now found that pure logic leads directly to this same model of reality, first through my mereological nihilism research, then thru by simulation theory research, and now through the new models of this book, which I now call _nonphysical Calvinism_. The model is about what reality looks like amid

[60] "Physical Reality is a Computer Simulation," University of Michigan – Dearborn, Humanities Winter Colloquium Lecture, April 10, 2013, University of Michigan-Dearborn, CASL Room 1030, 3 pm.
[61] Grupp, Jeff, 2019, March 17, God IS EVERYWHERE, Sermon, Pastor Jeff Grupp, 3-17-19, [Video File]. YouTube.com Channel: Praise and Love, URL: https://www.youtube.com/watch?v=PXXKEXg--XA.

the most direct level of experience of God, where merely being in a state of faith, automatically reveals God, in an experience an interaction that can be called *God-faith*.

7. Calvinist Metaphysics: Nonphysical Mind and Infinite God-Spirit

What Is Mind Really Experiencing?

We know from Chapter 1 that God is creating our inner minds, so that leads to a question: *Why wouldn't God, then, be filling our minds with mental contents (feelings, thoughts, and any mental contents), also?* We will see copious evidence, as this book unfolds, that that's what is going on, that is what our lives, in fact, *are*:

> *We know from Chapter 1 that our minds are creations of God, so how, then, do we avoid the conclusion that God is the creator of the contents of our minds? How do we avoid the idea that God creates our feelings, our thoughts?*

It seems unavoidable: if our minds are created by a creator-God, then the moment-to-moment thoughts, feelings, visualizations we have, would seem to be created not by a world around us, but rather are created by God, who creates, and therefore constructs, our minds.

And going a bit further with this: If God, being the Creator of all things (Revelation 4:11, Col. 1:16-17), is then *a lso* the creator of my mind, of my daily-life-experience, wherein He is filling my mind, my life, with predestined life-experience, why would there need to actually be an external world? *Wouldn't it be more efficient for an all-powerful creator-God to merely create*

(a) the experience in the mind, rather than (b) the experience in the mind + the 3D world that the experience maps?

Let me break that down in different words, because this is important. You live your life in the world believing that you are *directly* experiencing the world. But think about it more carefully, what are you really experiencing, the world itself, or your own mind-states? With some simple analysis, we can see that it's the second: you only experience your own mind, *not* the world itself. This will lead us into the conclusion that (a), and not (b), is correct. This has to do with what I call the theology of *fullness Calvinism*, or what I also call *nonphysical Calvinism*, which involves the most direct prayer and meditation to experience the presence of God.

When you see an apple on a table, for example, what are you really seeing? According to the standard view in academia—called the *realist* view—the idea of what is going on is typically as follows: you are seeing light that is reflected off of the apple's surface, the light enters your eyes, the information about the light travels via your optic nerve, to your primary visual cortex (PVC) in your brain, where an experience, a picture, is created in your brain by your PVC of the apple, by which you know the existence of the apple by. *But notice what was just said*: Where does your experience of the apple actually *happen*, on the table where the apple is located, or in your mind where the apple is not located? The answer is, of course, in your mind, where there is no apple, but only the fabricated picture, the map, of the apple that your mind has created. You don't experience the apple where it sits on the table, you experience the apple in your mind. In other words, you don't experience the apple directly, you experience only a mind-created map of it, picture of it, that your mind has created. But that means that you experience your own mind throughout your life (and perhaps some other minds that enter your mindspace, more on that below), and *not an external world*. As professional philosophers often put it: we are locked in our own experience our entire life, never seeing outside of it.

The ideas that led us to this finding are what is involved in the philosophy of *representationalism*, which is about how our experience of the world involves, roughly speaking, our own mind's inner map-making of an external world. This is the standard view of perception-and-reality held in academia. Popular films like *the Matrix* have nicely illustrated these ideas, and show how our daily lives could be just in the mind, without a real-world out there, where we may believe there is a world, but there is just the experience of the world with no world that creates our experiences, in fact, existing.

Representationalism is a very good and simple philosophy, but it has a truly *huge* consequence, that has rocked academia for hundreds of years (probably starting with John Locke's work in philosophy), and it's a consequence I have already eluded to above:

> *We don't know the apple directly, we only know the mind's experience, the mind's internally created picture, of the apple, so what reason do we really have, and how do we really know, that the apple is there beyond the experience of it?*

The answer is that there is <u>zero</u> reason, <u>zero</u> evidence, to know that the apple is there, beyond the experience of the apple, and few issues have been more central to academia, especially the field of philosophy, over the past centuries than this one. If a person *believes* the apple is there, outside oneself (notice I used the word "believes", not "knows"), they are what is called *a* **realist**: despite only experiencing reality in our minds, one nevertheless *believes* the outer reality still exists, roughly just as it is observed in the inner mind. Probably well over 99 percent of the world's population goes this direction. If a person does not follow the realist position, and instead says the apple must always remain an item of mental reality, not a physical item out in the world outside of mind, then one is what is called a **philosophical idealist**. Chapter 1 goes to the side of the philosophical idealist, much more evidence will be presented for showing that that is apparently the only option, and that Christianity also is solidly, strongly, in the philosophical idealist camp, as we will see. We humans are minds in a predestined computer program created by God. Far more evidence for this thesis, this theology—which I call **nonphysical Calvinism**—appears to exist, which shows that this could be what Christianity involves than the average Christian would ever guess.

Nonphysical Calvinism: Humans are Beings that are Spirit-Vessels in the Light of the Logos

This chapter and Chapter 10 contain information on what I call *nonphysical Calvinism*, or *fullness Calvinism*, and which can be considered an ultra-extreme version of Augustinian divine illumination theology (and almost could be called divine *implantation* theology), as well as a type of simulation theory. What I will present under the name of *nonphysical Calvinism* is a development from my work in simulation theory from the time I was teaching at the University of Michigan-Dearborn (see Grupp 2013). The information in this chapter and Chapter 9 follow directly from Chapter 1's man-is-a-spirit argument for the existence of God. Before I define nonphysical Calvinism and why I use this term "nonphysical Calvinism," let me give the reasons for why I hold the view, which are as follows:

1. God created and sustains nonphysical human minds (this comes from the man-is-a-spirit argument in Chapter 1), which, as stated above, leads to the conclusion that God, rather than the physical world, is where our mind content (our experience of daily life) comes from.

2. Combine what was just written in point 1 with the philosophy of representationalism just discussed in the previous section, and with that, not only is there extreme evidence for God being the cause of our colorful life-experience from moment to moment _rather than_ the world being the cause, _we furthermore do not have evidence for the existence of an external world_.

   Summing up points 1 and 2:

   We have extremely strong evidence for God as source of mind, and zero evidence for the existence of the world outside of us.

   You may be starting to see why nonphysical Calvinism is a vital theology.

3. God exists nonphysically, as a nonphysical Being: God is a Spirit (John 4:24), and any spirit is nonphysical. Human beings, being like God, in His image (Gen. 1:26), are more likely than not, for that very reason, to therefore _also_ have entirely nonphysical existence. Furthermore, God's entire being is spiritual, and thus nonphysical, and thus it would be hard to make sense of the idea that _our_ existence is physical and

nonspiritual, since that would mean we humans are in the *inverse* of the image of God, in those important, key ways, but that does not seem to be in-line with the Bible, that plainly tells us, we are in God's image. God lives completely in nonphysicality, being a Spirit, so how can't *we also* be in that sort of an image? Nonphysical Calvinism answers this. (Indeed, the very word "being" in the term human *being* denotes a likeness to the Creator, since the concept of being originally was intended to be different from *becoming*, where being was eternal and changeless (like God) and becoming involved change and was not eternal. This is why humans are called human *beings*, not human *becomings*, but in being human beings (human spirits), we are like God, not like nature. See Philippians 3:20.)

4. It has long been held in philosophy, since Descartes, that there is no bridge, no linkage, that is possible between nonphysical mind and a physical reality, since nonphysical and physical cannot interact with each other, and thus physical brain, body, and world, cannot interact with nonphysical mind. If this is correct, then only the nonphysical existence can be known, we *cannot* know a physical reality (since mind cannot link-up to anything physical to gather information about it), and this would serve as further evidence that the physical existence believed to be outside of the self is *only* an inner picture-screen, like a movie-screen in the mind, making it appear as if outer reality is real, but where it is only a movie-screen in the mind, or a *mindscreen* (hereafter I will call this **mindscreen**, or **mindscreen experience**). We know the nonphysical is real, since we know the mind is nonphysical via direct observation of it, but we also know we are *trapped*, so to speak, in the mind, and that we can cannot get outside of our own

experience. Therefore, we only have evidence of what is nonphysical, and any physical existence forever out of range of experience.

5. The Bible instructs us to live in holiness and _escape_ the physical reality (see the last section of this chapter), which is a direct instruction from God to live in nonphysicalist joy. Faith is constant belief in Christ that expands into being a constant communion with God, looking past the physical forms, to see the nonphysical One who is everywhere. Since the Bible presents this message, why would the physical world need to be an _actual_, physical-topological domain of mind-independent 3D matter objects, if we are just to see _past_ it at all moments of our lives?

6. In Chapter 2 above, we found that the definition of _evil_ is God's creation of the mind doing free will acts that specifically involve looking away from God and obsessing over creation (the physical domain). So, in other words, the very act of fixating on the created physical domain is the production of evil (or, in Old Testament language, "doing evil in the sight of the Lord"), so if that's the case, then how can we avoid the thesis that we are supposed to literally look _past_ the realness of the physical, directly to God-Creator, to bask in His light all the time? This is the message of nonphysical Calvinism.

7. Physical reality outside of the mind is describable by contradiction (subject of this chapter and chapters 8 and 10).

8. Several more reasons will be given in throughout the remainder of this book.

The basic idea of nonphysical Calvinism, then, most simply put, is that we humans are experiencing nonphysical minds, spirit-points, surrounded by the light of the Logos (Jesus Christ), where the physical world experienced exists as a screen in the mind, rather than an actual mind-independent reality of solids, liquids, and gasses "out there", outside of ourselves in a 3D or 4D spatial reality. I understand some will be turned-off by this direction in the book, but before making a judgment, please fully absorb this comment:

> *Perhaps what I call "nonphysical Calvinism" is not for everybody, but let me be clear:*
>
> > *for those who desire escape (Psalm 32:7) from this world of trouble (John 16:33) as soon as possible, who want to learn (Prov. 1:5) and follow evidence (2 Cor. 10:5), to learn the joyous art of not trusting self (2 Cor. 1:4), and transcending the disease of the self (2 Kings 8:38), by living in most-direct present-awareness of salvation in Christ (1 Sam. 2:1), most directly fixing their eyes on Jesus (Col. 3:1-2), for the most immediate, powerful experience of the presence of the Lord, to live in deepest faith-experience, and to really know how close God really is, then nonphysical Calvinism is the way to go for you.*

Now, let me go into nonphysical Calvinism further, where I will introduce it in this chapter, before going into it more deeply in later chapters.

Here is a definition and breakdown of nonphysical Calvinism, as I extract it from Scripture:

> A human person is a *vessel*: as in Acts 9:15, Paul is described as a *vessel* (KJV), so we know that is what people are, and from Chapter 1, and from point 3 above, earlier in this chapter, we know that we must be a *nonphysical* vessel. And we know from the simple dictionary definition of "vessel", that a vessel is a hollow container (see

Lamentations 4:2) that can be empty, but is for holding water, for example. A vessel is meant to be filled.

(i)   Since God is the Creator of all things (Rev. 4:11), *He then can only be the source of, the Creator of, the contents of our minds.* This is precisely in-line with point 1 at the start of this chapter. Therefore, it must be the case that God fills our minds (our moment-to-moment lives) with conscious contents: the experiences of our daily life are implanted in our minds by God).

(ii)   Also, the vessel *itself* can *also* be filed by God *Himself* (indwelling of the Holy Spirit), wherein when God *fills* the vessel it becomes a living soul (Gen. 2:7), and where without God's infilling the vessel is not a living soul (it is a non-soul).

The vessel-self is a like a specific and individual mold, die-cast, form (see Isaiah 64:8, Romans 9:21, Lamentations 4:2, etc.), for lack of better words, and which is also something like a nonphysical computer that God created before time, created after His own image, and which has an exact *name.*

Christ is everywhere/omnipresent, infinite in every direction, surrounding and holding selves/vessels (Col. 1:16-17). A person's life is God's programmed and predestined inflow and implanting of conscious contents into the vessel that form the theater of life-experience (the mindscreen), which a person is either enslaved to, or, at times, interacts with via their free will.

When a nonphysical vessel (human self) is a living soul (the vessel is filled with the Logos), it can experience (become aware of) itself, to varying degrees and intensities, as resting in omnipresent-God.

What has been written so far in this chapter leads to the idea that our reality, our existence in this world, which we believe is a 3D physical reality outside of ourselves, is in fact no more than a cinema in the mind, like a virtual reality world in the mind, that we humans live-in together and share, by God implanting our vessels with conscious contents, which causes us to live together in what is roughly like virtual reality worlds, testing grounds of God, and meant to be broken-out-of in order to live in the joy of the Lord (Neh. 8:10, Ps. 16:11). We have no evidence to believe our existence is anything that exists outside of our minds, the logic of God-Christ appears to be in-line with these findings, and the spiritual implications of nonphysical Calvinism are momentous, in their capacity to get us into direct relationship with Christ, and directly in the presence of God, for the following reason:

> When one follows the Bible and makes meditation on the Lord their non-nonsense daily project, their *primary objective* (Psalm 48:9, etc.), fixing their eyes on Jesus (Hebrews 12:2, etc.), understanding that they are commanded to seek God's face constantly (Psalm 105:4, etc.), where the Son is the radiance of God's glory (Hebrews 1:3), while simultaneously understanding that our reality is in accord with the points written in this chapter so far, *one will, in times of meditation in Christ, most powerfully, directly, witness the infinite light of the Logos behind, empowering, and within all things*, in every direction of the mindscreen of your daily life that you look. This is truly the experience every person needs, to power their daily life, and which can be used to

truly catapult a person into the day-to-day life of ministry and living as a slave for Christ.

So, in summary, the following illustration should indicate more of what your life is like, according to nonphysical Calvinism:

> You and a friend of yours, for example, both have an experience when you are, for example, having lunch. You believe you are together in a physical world, by living in your physical bodies, being directly together in that way, in a spatial reality filled with matter objects. But in reality, what is going on, according to nonphysical Calvinism, is each you and your friend are interacting in the screens of your minds _only_: your bodies, the world around you, all you see that you believe is outside of yourself is actually merely part of the the screen of your mind (analogous to the idea of virtual reality experience in your consciousness), where you are implanted with experience, by God, of being with your friend in that specific setting, and she is of you, also, in that specific setting. You are each experiencing mindscreens, interacting with each other because you each have experience of one another implanted into your mindscreens by God, rather than by an external world. It is not that you and your reality do not exist, or that your situation of having lunch is not real. Rather, it is merely that the two of you do not have an ontology quite like believe: you interact in the screens of your mind, not in a world of spatiotemporal existence. Each of you are nonphysical mind-points, surrounded by and possibly even indwelt by the infinite and omnipresent light of Christ.

Again, more evidence than what has already been presented will be given for the thesis of nonphysical Calvinism below, and we will also explore why this theology can, specifically, be called *Calvinist*, which is, in my opinion, certainly the theology most closely matching Scripture. But let's first explore point 5 above, which shows that the physical world is only describable in terms of contradiction, and thus cannot actually exist, as a real mind-independent[62] entity outside of consciousness.

Holiness and Nonphysicality: The Meaning of Life is *Seeing God*

Holiness, in Christian theology, is being set apart in order to be like God. This means that if God is nonphysical, we are to be like God, and we are to be the nonphysical created beings that we are. As we were discussing at the start of Chapter 3, breaking past the veil of the physical forms, to have our eyes fixed on the nonphysical One, the Maker-Logos, all the time, is what we are instructed to do. In this book, we will take this to be what is meant by the term "holiness". We are to be of God, who is omnipresent Power, that is nonphysical, and we are to exist in a state of faith-awareness of that omnipresent One all the time. A verse of utter importance to this issue is:

Hebrews 12:14 King James Version (KJV)

---

[62] What I mean by mind-independent is that something exists regardless if there is a mind to think about it or not. For example, imagine that atoms are colorless, but the apple that is made of atoms is red, then where does the redness come from? It cannot come from the atoms or any arrangement of the atoms. And there is no accumulation of the atoms where at redness emerges where previously there was on redness. For this reason, the redness would be believed to be created by the mind: the specific way that the atoms appear to the human sensorium prompts the human brain-mind system to create an experience of redness. In this case, the redness would exist mind-dependently: independent of the mind, the apple is colorless since the atoms are colorless (mind-independently the apple is colorless), but the mind creates a color experience when it forms an image of the apple in mind (mind-dependently, the apple is red).

14 Follow peace with all men, and holiness, without which no man shall see the Lord:

Notice how this verse tells us to *follow* holiness, so we *go* where God *is*, that is the task of our life, the meaning of our life. This is not future tense writing, but present-tense—this is what we are to do *now*. So, holiness is not something to partake in only *after* physical bodily death, for if it were, why did Paul write Galatians 2:20 in *past* tense, and Philippians 1:21 in present tense? Answer: because holiness is the meaning of life for created beings *now*, as declared in both the Old Testament (OT) and the New (NT):

Leviticus 20:8 (NIV)

[8] Keep my decrees and follow them. I am the LORD, who makes you holy.

Luke 17:21 (KJ V)

[21] Neither shall they say, Lo here! or, lo there! for, behold, the kingdom of God is within you.

And notice that Hebrews 12:14 indicates that holiness is the avenue to *seeing God*. Since so many of the Bible characters had *direct* experience of God (Moses, Ezekiel, etc.), including all of the people who interacted with Jesus in the Gospels, we have to interpret "see God" in Hebrews 12:14 as meaning that is our task in life, the meaning of life, *now*. That is why Hannah said, in the Old Testament, she was in God's salvation in the present tense:

1 Samuel 2:1 King J ames Version (KJ V)

2 And Hannah prayed, and said, My heart rejoiceth in the Lord, mine horn is exalted in the Lord: my mouth is enlarged over mine enemies; because I rejoice in thy salvation.

Holiness is seeing omnipresent God-Logos behind the cover of the physical, the shield of the physical.

The attributes of holiness show us that our spiritual existence is a *nonphysical existence*. In Hebrew, "holiness" comes from the *qodesh* word family, and "[t]he semitic origin of this noun is… lost in the mists of ancient obscurity" (Greathouse 1998, 12). The term denotes "the very nature of Deity" (Ibid.). Our Diety, Jesus Christ, invites us to participate in holiness, *partaking of it*.

> 2 Peter 1:4 King James Version (KJV)
>
> 4 Whereby are given unto us exceeding great and precious promises: that by these ye might be partakers of the divine nature, having escaped the corruption that is in the world through lust.

The wording of this verse is of utter importance to the theology of nonphysical Calvinism being developed in this book, and this verse cannot be underestimated. We are told that our task is to partake in divinity, and the cause of that is *escaping* the physical domain. Notice that word choice: *escaping*. Is it present tense, and a verb. This is what we are to be doing all the time: escaping physical reality. This equation is unmistakable, perfectly clear. *Nonphysical Calvinism is the most intense theology in instructing on how to escape the physical*. All other theologies do not get the job done, and they compromise with 2 Peter 1:4. As we will discuss in this part of the book, nonphysical Calvinism greatly *lessens the realness of the physical*, and that is one of the direct methods for having ever-present faith-experience in Christ, where the realness of the world is diminished to a mindscreen, as discussed below.

Humans are a spirit, more like the nonphysical supernaturality of Yahweh than like a hunk of unholy matter, and the fallenness of our life and this world has tricked us into believing we are mere flesh, when we were created as, and still are, _spirit_. The qualities of holiness are the _qualities of God_. If we have the Mind of Christ (Phil. 2:5), we take on these holy qualities: this his a causal equation: have Christ's mind as our mind and then we are caused to have holiness. We do not do the works in us, God does them (John 14:10). But this means we are to _escape_ the physical (2 Pet. 1:4), which is a heavy Biblical topic (Psalm 32:7, etc.), but almost undiscussed among Christians worldwide. To escape the physical is to _break free from_, _avoid_ (dictionary definitions) the physical. This means our minds should be free of, avoiding, the physical, and combining that with our discussion of faith in chapter 5, our eyes our fixed on Jesus. We are instructed in the Bible to live a fully nonphysical existence, and to _be_ this, as nonphysical Calvinism involves, requires our belief in the realness of the physical to be lessened.

In escaping the world, the qualities of God's holiness obtained, are, as Greathouse discusses: mystery, unapproachability, energy, consuming fire, spiritual drunkenness, otherness (being _set apart_ [Greathouse 1998, 16-17, 28]; also see Lev 20:8 in the ISV), separation from humans and human ways of understanding, prerational and numinous (beyond rational analysis), evoking feelings of awe (_mysterium trenemdum_), glory, burning splendor, purity, divine activity, innerness (holiness is more of _innerness_ [nonphysical, spiritual, mental, mind-like] than outerness [physicality], not like unholy matter), and holiness is the innermost quality of God (Greathouse 1998, 12-17). Greathouse writes, citing Mullenberg and Sellen: holiness is "the innermost reality to which all others are related," "the deepest and innermost nature of God..." (See Greathouse 1998, 16)

It is important to know that all these qualities can only be a *single* quality, as Greathouse discussed, as God does not have parts, but is *One*. (In medieval philosophy, this is called the Doctrine of Divine Simplicity.) This is why conceptualization of God's qualities is not possible for us, and transcends all understanding (Phil. 4:7). God is to be experience, as an understandable mystery (Col. 2:2).

Work Cited

Greathouse, William M, 1998, *Wholeness in Christ: Toward a Biblical Theology of Holiness*, Kansas City: Beacon Hill Press.

8. The Implantation Argument: A New Proof for the Existence of God

Introduction

In this chapter, I will present a new proof for the existence of a creator-God, which I call _The Implantation Argument for the Existence of God_, and there are multiple forms of it that will be presented in this chapter and later in chapter 10. In general, _The Implantation Argument for the Existence of God_ shows that the physical reality is only describable in terms of contradiction, and/or the physical reality cannot exist as an actual mind-independent entity, and if not, then the conscious contents of one's daily life can only be described (as with the man-is-a-spirit argument) as coming from a source that is _not_ the world. The Implantation Argument leads directly to nonphysical Calvinism. Chapter 1 and Chapter 7 showed that the contents of daily experience can only be had by implantation of mind and mind-contents directly from God (mind and experience is created from moment-to-moment by God), and in Chapter 10 it will be shown with yet a different argument that the only logical option is that our conscious daily life experience can only be the result of being implanted by another mind, another intelligence, which is an all-powerful, infinite intelligence (God-Christ). The argument can be presented in three ways, as follows:

1. Everything that is observed externally is, in fact, partless atoms.

2. What I experience externally is not partless atoms, and cannot be reduced-down-to partless atoms, or be created by mindless, undirected atoms.

3. <u>Conclusion</u>: External reality I experience is not caused by an external reality; my mind-contents about externality are implanted in me (in my mind) by something other than by externality.

1. External reality, containing spatiality and extended objects that are in motion and persist through time, reduces to mereological nihilism.

2. What I experience externally is not partless atoms, and cannot be reduced-down-to partless atoms, or be created by mindless, undirected atoms.

3. <u>Conclusion</u>: External reality I experience is not caused by an external reality; my mind-contents about externality are implanted in me (in my mind) by something other than by externality.

1. External reality is only describable in terms of contradiction.

2. The external reality I experience cannot exist mind-independently.

3. <u>Conclusion</u>: External reality I experience is not caused by an external reality; my mind-contents about externality are implanted in me (in my mind) by something other than by externality.

Essentially, what these three arguments, that all arrive at the same conclusion, involve, is the idea that

If we analyze the most fundamental rudiments of the observed reality outside of us (motion, spatiality, extension, solidity, atomism, etc.), each of those rudimentary aspects simply and obviously lead to inescapable conflict with what we experience (the description of the rudimentary elements on the one hand, and the raw experience we have of reality on the other, do not line up, and seriously conflict—e.g., reality is atoms but we see extensions that have opposite properties as atoms and which therefore cannot be described as being composed of atoms), and lead to obvious and inescapable contradiction: the description of the rudiments of reality are contradictory, and thus cannot exist mind-independently.

When we look out at our reality, we see extended matter. We can divide it down to small parts we cannot see. The question is can we divide extended chunks of physical reality all the way down to partless atoms (Greek atoms, philosophical atoms)[63], or not.

1. If yes, then the partless atoms are unchanging entities. I consider these atoms to be unchanging for a few reasons, such as because they don't have parts, and without parts they cannot alter, such as by having varying internal arrangements. Also, for those reasons, partless atoms also would seem to be unchanging, eternal, and uncaused.

2. If no, then we never arrive at partless extended matter. In the second case, reality is always extended, where any extension is divisible, and has parts.

---

[63] These are not the atoms that scientists discuss, which are composed of parts (electrons, quarks), but rather what I mean by *philosophical atoms* are what the ancient Greeks referred to as "atoms," which are the true irreducible building blocks of reality, which are partless basic buildings blocks of reality. Professional philosophers who discuss these basic building blocks refer to them by the names simples, partless atoms, basic building blocks, quantum abstract atoms, and Greek atoms.

Point 1 would, I surmise, be very appealing to atheists, since eternal and unchanging atoms would apparently be uncreated, and, atheists believe, such would absolutely eliminate the need for a monotheistic creator-God since, as the ancient Greek atomist Democritus appeared to maintain, point 1 coherently describes how human macroscopic experience of the world could be changing, and beginningless, but without any need for a creator-God. This was considered by some as a great step forward in Greek philosophy, since it avoided the problem of change:

> The problem of change:
>
> If object O has properties a, b, c, and d, at time t_1, and then at time t_2 has properties a, b, c, and e, wherein d is replaced by e: O = [a, b, c, d] is distinct from O* = [a, b, c, e], such as when an apple (O) changes from being fresh to rotten (O*), or changes from being not dented (O) to dented (O*), where O is *different* at O*, so that O ≠ O*, and therefore the first object (O) must cease to exist and a new entity/object (O*) must come into existence.

With the *problem of change*, if an entity changes, it is no longer the original entity, it is a *new* entity. A bike, B, if considered a single whole (a single thing), is not the same as when run over by a car, there the bike is in a new state, B*. Humans will want to say that B=B*, but this is like saying

> unsmashed bike = smashed bike,

or like saying

> red apple = brown apple.

But these are contradictions, so it appears that we have to say that

> bike ≠ smashed bike,

red apple ≠ brown apple.

But this means that the smashed bike, and the brown/rotting apple, are not the same entity, which would mean that they have no continuous existence with the unsmashed bike and red apple respectively—but that would require that the smashed bike and the brown/rotting apple "pop into existence," as new entities.

> Parmenides had argued that it is impossible for there to be change without something coming from nothing. Since the idea that something could come from nothing was generally agreed to be impossible, Parmenides argued that change is merely illusory. In response, Leucippus and Democritus, along with other Presocratic pluralists such as Empedocles and Anaxagoras, developed systems that made change possible by showing that it does not require that something should come to be from nothing. These responses to Parmenides suppose that there are multiple unchanging material principles, which persist and merely rearrange themselves to form the changing world of appearances. In the atomist version, these unchanging material principles are indivisible particles, the atoms: the atomists are often thought to have taken the idea that there is a lower limit to divisibility to answer Zeno's paradoxes about the impossibility of traversing infinitely divisible magnitudes... (Berryman 2016, Sect. 2)

Point 2 involves the idea that extended matter involves *infinite divisibility*: much like any extended piece of the real number line can be split with infinite divisions, but where in dividing, one can never arrive at a last division, and at an *unextended* segment of the number line[64], the same can be said of extended matter, where there is no need to believe reality can be divided down to the partless philosophical atoms. (I argued in a previous article [Grupp 2006] that mind-independent extended matter is impossible, and all empirical reality reduces to partless atoms, a position called *mereological nihilism*.)

Infinite divisibility involves the concept that extended is *divisible* extended matter, where the divisions of the extended matter are mind-independent, and therefore the infinite division steps exist mind-independently in the extended matter, regardless if a person thinks about them or not. For this reason, extended matter should be referred to as infinitely *divided*, not infinitely divisible. "Infinitely divisible" could be interpreted as meaning that some of the infinite divisions of matter have not been done yet (the Greek philosophers, Aristotle, seemed to hold that sort of a view), rather than the divisions already existing, and the matter being already divided. This is a critical point, and ultimate shows why point 2 reduced to point 1: or, in other words, why anti-atomism reduces down to atomism. The reason we need to discuss this in detail is because it has been believed for thousands of years in philosophy that point 2, atomless infinite divisibility is a contender to point 1, philosophical atomism—as if either theory could end-up being the correct theory of ultimate reality, since purportedly nobody had settled the issue yet, or not, on which was the correct view. I have analyzed these positions for years, and they were the main topic of my MA work, and I think there is a

---

[64] In other words, if I were to start dividing the span from 0 to 1 on the real number line, starting at .5, then at .25, then .125, and so forth, I will never arrive at a last division, and there will always be another division step, to where I can divide, so an unextended (atomic) piece of the number line is never arrived at.

hitherto undiscussed reason to claim atomism is correct, and atomless infinite divisibility cannot describe observable reality.

When we divide an extended matter object—say, for example, a smooth surface of water—as we divide the water surface into smaller and smaller segments we will arrive at the level of the water molecule. We can continue diving after that, wherein we will divide into either smaller molecule segments, or into atoms (and by that I mean the atoms scientists refer to, which have parts [electron, proton, etc.], not the Greek atoms, or philosophical atoms discussed above[65]). Notice that we don't say that we have *created* the atoms by our dividing the molecule, but rather, *the atoms already existed, separate and divided*, and our dividing up the molecule, and therein considering its parts, is merely a way of discussing divisions of reality *that already existed*. In this way, we don't imagine that in dividing up reality we are *creating divisions*, but rather, they already exist. If I cut a hunk of meat, I am merely separating its cells in a specific location, and in the cases where I cut right down the middle of a cell, in that case I am merely separating organelles and such. And when I divide the organelles into molecules, and the molecules into scientific atoms, in each case, I am not creating divisions—*the divisions already existed*. In other words, *mind-independent matter is already infinitely divided*, which is a key point. All the infinite division steps already exist in any extended chunk of matter, and it is better referred to as infinite *divided* extended matter, rather than infinitely divisible extended matter.

---

[65] The word "atom" is used in academia in two ways: to describe a unit of composite matter, which are the atoms that scientist discuss, and the unit of partless reality, or philosophical atoms (Greek, atoms), which philosophers discuss.

Some professional philosophers have claimed that infinitely divisible matter can be referred to as being *atomless* (non-atomic matter), wherein it can be forever divided when one starts dividing from an extended surface. This is indeed correct, but that is not the issue just discussed in the previous paragraph. They are considering matter as being in something like a division *potential*: If one were to divide an extension of matter, one can keep dividing and dividing, never reaching a last division, as discussed above.

But it is more precise to consider how, also as discussed above, all the divisions already exist, and when one divides matter, one can only ever be merely separating chunks of matter along preexisting division lines. So, the question is this: along the preexisting, mind-independent divisions of extended matter, do we compare this to the divisibility of the Real number line? The number line is a collection of extensions that are divisible but also divided, but that logically leads to the number line being a set of point-sized (sizeless) regions on the number line. Would extended matter be any different? If extended matter obeys the mathematics of the Real number line, then how could extended matter and the extended Real number line be any different from one another? How could extended matter non-mathematically deviate from the mathematics of the Real line? But if extended matter is actually infinitely divided matter, then extended matter is a type of atomism (point 1 above), as I will discuss shortly, and point 2 (atomless infinite divisibility) would be incorrect: observable reality would be describable only as being atomic.

The discussion at hand, then, moves to only being about atomism, and all of observable reality being composed of philosophical atoms. The only questions remaining would be if the philosophical atoms composing reality

A. If they are point-sized (sizeless) or if they have a partless extension.

B. Are eternal and unchanging or not.

As for point A, let us call extended philosophical atoms by the term _Democritean atoms_[66], I argued previously (Grupp 2006, 2013) that only point-sized philosophical atoms exist, and Democritean atoms are impossible, and I will discuss this a bit more below.

And as for B, in proving the existence of God, if the atoms are non-eternal, or are changing, this points to the existence of God. I say this because if a partless item changes, as the problem of change above indicated, atoms would have to be coming into existence _ex nihilo_ and/or by a "source "outside of the realm of atoms—outside of the realm of naturalistic reality—which is the definition of God[67]. So if philosophical atoms are non-eternal and changing, rather than unchanging and eternal, the existence of God is apparently already proven, by atoms flashing in-and-out of existence[68]. So, for proving the existence of God, we can put on the shelf any discussion of

---

[66] The phrase "Democritean atoms", is used by many; see, for example, Hoffman and Rosenkranntz (1997 13, 150-151), among others. See Hoffman, Joshua, and Rosenkranntz, Gary S, 1997, _Substance: Its Nature and Existence_, New York: Routledge, pp. 13 150-151.

[67] This would perhaps be in-line, or somewhat in-line, with an occasionalistic creator-God, which is a scenario where all direct causation is originated by a monotheistic creator God. Christianity may very well be in-line with occasionalistic theology and philosophy.

[68] Interestingly, this is precisely what quantum physicists observe in the experimental setting. This is the standard position in quantum physics. Consider what famous physicist, George Kane says:

> Nearly all particles are unstable and decay into others. The word decay has a technical meaning in physics—one particle disappears, typically turning into two or three others. A major difference between the way decay is used in physics and its use in everyday life or biology is that the particles that characterize the final state are not in any sense already in the decaying particle. The initial particle really disappears, and the final particles appear. The photons that make up the light we see provide an example: The photons emitted from a light bulb when it is turned on are not particles that were in the bulb just waiting to come out, and photons that enter our eyes... are absorbed by the molecules in our eyes and disappear. All particles can be created or absorbed in interactions with other particles. (Kane, George. 2000. _Supersymmetry_. Cambridge: Perseus Publishing, page 19.)

changing and noneternal philosophical atoms, and we only need consider the scenario where philosophical atoms are eternal and unchanging.

The point is that either way, with A or B, any situation of philosophical atomism will arrive at a creator-God creating conscious experience of reality: what we see and know can only be the result of a creator-God bringing that is beyond being, bringing our conscious contents into existence. This is because the reality of atomism—whether eternal or noneternal, changing or unchanging, Democritean or point-sized, our experience of the external world around us, outside of us, is the opposite of what can exist by any sort of philosophical atomism, wherein conclusion 1 is arrived at: *External reality I experience is not caused by an external reality; my mind-contents about externality are implanted not by externality.*

I say that because if atoms are point-sized, then, as has been well-known since the time of the Greek Presocratic philosopher Zeno, the atoms are invisible, and no accumulation of them can result in them being anything but invisible. Putting that in a different way, point-sized atoms have no size, and therefore no surface by which they can be viewed/observed, or by which they can interact with one another. Not only can they *not* accumulate into an extended surface because they have no dimensionality (size) that can accumulate, further, without having touching surface that can interact, they therefore *cannot* interact with each other to form accumulations which, in turn, form the structures of the physical world. So, if point-sized philosophical atoms were what makes up physical reality, then conscious experience of the mind of a human could not be caused by the external world, and content from another source would have to be implanted into mind in order for consciousness to exist.

So, all that is left is eternal and unchanging Democritean atoms composing reality. This position involves the insurmountable problem of how to describe a partless, seamless, uncuttable, undivided but *extended* philosophical atom. In simpler terms: how can a philosophical atom have a size but not parts? We are left with questions such as: If a Democritean atom is spherical, how *can't* it have a top and bottom half. This should be seen as absurdity—game over—but understandably, there is tremendous desire for academics to try to explain how philosophical atoms can have extension, so to avoid the Zeno's Measure Paradox (which leads to nonphysical Calvinism and to simulation theory), which is the problem of trying to explain how extended matter can be created by zero-dimensional sizeless philosophical atoms. This has been the entire motivation for the physics of string theory.

There are many attempts to explain how Democritean atoms (also called "extended simples") can actually make sense. The reader can go and research these at length, but I don't see how any of them overcome the fundamental and seemingly obvious problems with them that I pointed out in Grupp 2006, and most completely later in Grupp 2013:

The Anti-Democritean Argument:

If this is a Democritean atom, a basic building block, which has no parts, but has a size, such as in this picture:

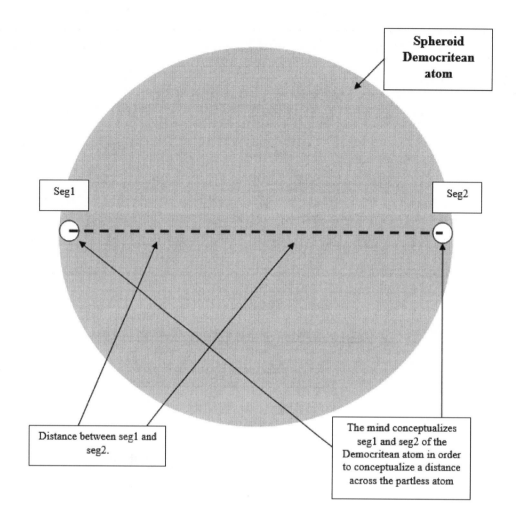

Spheroid Democritean atom

Seg1

Seg2

Distance between seg1 and seg2.

The mind conceptualizes seg1 and seg2 of the Democritean atom in order to conceptualize a distance across the partless atom

[This picture appeared in Grupp 2006, p. 322.]

About this picture, in Grupp 2013 I stated that

> This Democritean atom cannot be changing in any way, since changing would represent a rearrangement of parts, but the Democritean atom does not have any parts. So, the only way you can describe the Democritean atom is by its fundamental feature, its size, represented by the dashed line, which is *the distance across the Democritan atom*. But what is distance? It is the noncoinciding of two things that are non-identical... Nothing is at a distance from itself. Distance is when you have distinct things: different things that don't

coincide, where between them the mind sees a "gap" [represented by the dashed line, above]. This is specifically what a Democritean atom, a partless extended philosophical atom, *cannot have*. Why? Because in order to describe distance from any "here" to any "there", you have to have two non-identical pieces which are non-coinciding. But this Democritean atom does not have any nonidentical pieces, and you can't say there are two distinct aspects of it, from "here" to "here", for example [pointing to Seg1 and Seg2], because this Democirtean atom is only point pieces—what philosophers call one improper part, so therefore, any description of it has to describe all of it, the whole thing. So you can't start talking about a distinct piece *here* [pointing to Seg1], and a distinct piece here [pointing to Seg2], in order to define a distance across a Democirtean atom. The point is that the Democritean atom is something that absolutely requires a concept of size or distance in its definition and description, but where this sort of description is impossible. So, the Democritean atom is a contradiction and does not exist.[69] (Grupp 2013)

If there are no Democritean regions of *irreducible* (non-divisible) partless, extended solidity in any chuck of matter, since, like the number line, matter is infinitely divided, then the extended matter could only represent a continuum of infinite point-atoms (what I called quantum abstract atoms in

---

[69] Grupp 2013, https://www.youtube.com/watch?v=dyAmY6QAcDU, starting at 44:15 into the talk at the University of Michigan – Dearborn. This part of the talk, from 44-47 minutes, was an attempt to discuss the problems with Democritean atoms in simplest terms. For a more information on this argument, see Grupp 2006.
Currently, in academia, there is great popularity to discuss Democritean philosophical (partless) atoms, by names such as string theory, Plank times (smallest unit of time, 10^{-43}), and so on. The problems with Democritean atoms discussed here will apply to those as well, and those Democritean regions cannot exist. There is a long history of physicists believing they have arrived at the last unit of irreducible matter, and where that matter had temporal or spatial extension, only to time out that they could divide further.

Grupp 2006). Another way to say this is: if there are no Democritean solids (extended simples, extended philosophical atoms), then all infinitely divided matter is in fact sizeless points, since just like the real number line, which is infinitely divided, wherein Zeno's Measure Paradox sets in, and external reality cannot exist as we believe it does. From this point, nonphysical Calvinism would be needed to make sense of our moment-to-moment experience.

Time, matter, and space, all would be susceptible to the arguments of this chapter, and all would not involve coherent extensions: no extensions of itme (duration), of matter (surface extension), or space (topological extension).

This is but one way that external reality cannot be explained in noncontradictory fashion, and thus cannot coherently exist. What has been described in this chapter is a description of Zeno's Measure Paradox. But the ancient Greek philosopher, Zeno, had many more ways of describing reality in terms of contradiction. And these are not surreal, roundable, remote explanation problems about the reality we observe, but rather, simple and fundamental contradictions about reality are seem to be built into the very bedrock of reality. With all we have seen so far in this book, how do we avoid do we avoid the conclusion of nonphysical Calvinism, which I will discuss more in the next chapter.

Works Cited

Berryman, Sylvia, "Democritus", *The Stanford Encyclopedia of Philosophy* (Winter 2016 Edition), Edward N. Zalta (ed.), URL = <https://plato.stanford.edu/archives/win2016/entries/democritus/>.

Lycan, William, "Representational Theories of Consciousness", *The Stanford Encyclopedia of Philosophy* (Summer 2015 Edition), Edward N. Zalta (ed.), URL = <https://plato.stanford.edu/archives/sum2015/entries/consciousness-representational/>.

Grupp, Jeff, 2018, "Sin, Nothingness, the Liar Paradox, and the Contamination of Creation," in *Theologic: Revelation, Calvinism, Surrender, Nothingness*, Kalamazoo: Praise and Love Church, pages 32-54 print copy available at Lulu.com, free online copy at Praiseandlove.net).

Grupp, Jeff, 2018b, "God's Pre-Election Knowledge of the Soul: A New Interpretation of Biblical Election and Predestination Showing Why God Only Chose Some Rather Than All," in *Theologic: Revelation, Calvinism, Surrender, Nothingness*, Kalamazoo: Praise and Love Church, pages 5-31, (print copy available at Lulu.com, free online copy at Praiseandlove.net).

Grupp, Jeff, 2013, "Physical Reality is a Computer Simulation," University of Michigan – Dearborn, Humanities Winter Colloquium Lecture, April 10, 2013, University of Michigan-Dearborn, CASL Room 1030, 3 pm. Can be heard thru this link: https://www.youtube.com/watch?v=dyAmY6QAcDU.

Grupp, Jeffrey, 2006, "Mereological Nihilism: Quantum Atomism and the Impossibility of Material Constitution," *Axiomathes: An International Journal in Ontology and Cognitive Systems*, Vol. 16, No. 3, pp. 245-386.

9. Deep Calvinist Metaphysics as Direct Communion with Christ

How is Nonphysical Calvinism *Calvinistic*?

Why I label nonphysical Calvinism as a species of *Calvinism* will be briefly discussed next. This analysis will begin to show us the meditative and prayerful benefits of the logical discoveries of this book. Speaking somewhat humorously, but also to make a point, if the theology of Kart Barth can be considered *Calvinistic*, then there will be little problem fitting the theology of nonphysical Calvinism into the overall theology of Calvinism.

If one extracts and discovers the broad themes and philosophies of the Bible, it is my assertion that one comes to a theology that is in-line with the Augustinian-Calvinist framework. And it has been my project to dig *deeper* into Calvinist theology to uncover more of what Scripture involves. I would assert that what I have written in this book is within the framework, the bounds, of Calvinist theology, where this book is a continuation of previous work I have done (see Grupp 2018a, 2018b, 2019b) on deepening and expanding Calvinist theology, as is greatly needed.

Most broadly put, Calvinism is the theology where God has the most control over reality, creating all souls before time[70], placing this in a reality that is

---

[70] I have previously discussed how I believe this is the Calvinist position—more specifically, that for Scriptural reasons, Calvinism must involve this view, which is a theological position, associated with the theology of supralapsarianism, where God creates all souls before time (many Scriptures mention this pre-time creating of humans, such as Eph. 1:4). I discussed this at length of Grupp 2018a, and also to some degree in Grupp 2018b.

preplanned by God, where some souls are created to be salvific, and the rest created to be destroyed, in a reality controlled like a preplanned computer program (with a bit of free-will involved), all for the glory of God. Denominations have been created just out of a reaction against Calvinism (such as the denominations of Arminianism), but if one denies the supposed controlled and planned computer program-like reality we live in—a computer program created by God—consider the following passage, about the all-important time leading right up to the Second coming of Jesus:

> Zechariah 14:1-4 New King James Version (NKJV)
> 14 Behold, the day of the Lord is coming,
> And your spoil will be divided in your midst.
> 2 For I will gather all the nations to battle against Jerusalem;
> The city shall be taken,
> The houses rifled,
> And the women ravished.
> Half of the city shall go into captivity,
> But the remnant of the people shall not be cut off from the city.
> 3 Then the Lord will go forth
> And fight against those nations,
> As He fights in the day of battle.
> 4 And in that day His feet will stand on the Mount of Olives,
> Which faces Jerusalem on the east.
> And the Mount of Olives shall be split in two,
> From east to west,
> Making a very large valley;
> Half of the mountain shall move toward the north
> And half of it toward the south.

There are so many passages like this in the Bible, showing the careful pre-planning of reality, especially things like the crucifixion (see Acts 2:23) and eschaton. The planning is about events beyond our control, beyond our understanding.

Now let's explore nonphysical Calvinism in more detail.

God's Sovereignty and Grace

Calvinism is the theology of the Bible that involves God having the *fullest* control over reality, as compared to other theologies. There are references to there being some chance events that exist, according to the Old Testament, which are still in God's control since He *allows* them to exist, but in general, the level of control God has is direct and *total*—for example, even any chance events that exist are nevertheless *allowed by God to exist* as events of chance, and thus are still under God's control. Consider how much control God has over His Creation in these passages in Job:

> Job 37:14-16 New International Version (NIV)

> 14 "Listen to this, Job; stop and consider God's wonders. 15 Do you know how God controls the clouds and makes his lightning flash?

> 16 Do you know how the clouds hang poised, those wonders of him who has perfect knowledge?

This is the first reason that I call nonphysical Calvinism a *Calvinist* theology: what I have defined as nonphysical Calvinism gives God the maximum control over His Creation. For example, if the very contents of our minds are formed and placed into our minds, giving us the fullness of life, with brilliant colors everywhere in our view, filled with and intermixed with our feelings, with our hopes and dreams, yearnings, thoughts, and imaginings—all of which are creations of God, in a life that is in the sunlight of God's grace, where only bits of our free-will that very sparsely exist, *that* is a theology which most fully adheres to the concept that God is in control *of all*, the predestinating God that is Maker of *all things*.

God Revealed Through (Violations of) Nature

Another reason that what I call nonphysical Calvinism is a *Calvinist* theology is because, with Calvinist theology, we are expected to have revelation of Jesus Christ *continually*, as He continually creates and reveals Himself by and through *nature* (Creation). In the *Institutes of Christian Religion*, Calvin wrote: "Wherever you cast your eyes… there is no spot in the universe wherein you cannot discern at least some sparks of God's glory." (Cited in Hesselink 2012, 5).

A key principle of Calvinist theology is that the ongoing production of Creation, by God, occurring through the Logos (Christ Jesus), through Creation and via predestination. Regarding the former, Romans 1:20 is often noted as the verse God's revelation through Creation:

Romans 1:20 New International Version (NIV)

20 For since the creation of the world God's invisible qualities—his eternal power and divine nature—have been clearly seen, being understood from what has been made, so that people are without excuse.

Romans 1:20 King James Version (KJV)

20 For the invisible things of him from the creation of the world are clearly seen, being understood by the things that are made, even his eternal power and Godhead; so that they are without excuse.

It is difficult to know precisely what Calvin meant by, for example, the quote above that is in John Hesselink's book. Let me give two possible interpretations of what it might mean (one interpretation I will strongly agree with as Scriptural, and the other I would argue is heresy):

- Interpretation of Calvin's quote #1: When I see the majesty of nature, I see God, I know Him by His amazing Creation. When I see that sunrise, I know God is real.
- Interpretation of Calvin's quote #2: When I see the of any object of nature, I sense infinite Power deep within it, behind it, powering and fueling it, creating it, giving it its existence moment-to-moment.

From what I've read, I believe Calvin adhered to something more like the top bullet-point, but in my opinion, the second one is fact (i.e., a mystical experience we can directly have), and the top is incorrect.

But moving on from this discrepancy, nature is a catalyst to have experience of God, in the sense the lower bullet-point indicates: nature's ways are a way to experience God, in the sense that we can see the Power behind nature, that is in everything. This experience is such that one should fix their eyes on omnipresent Christ to the point that the forms of nature take the appearance of merely being a screen (mindscreen), since they lose their realness as compared to the power of the Lord one has awareness of within and behind all the forms of the natural world, of the mindscreen. I have had moments where I look straight at God-all-around, the light of Christ radiating the Father (Heb. 1:3), where physical reality will appear to blink-out at (particularly joyous) times. So, in this sense, that God is seen in all things (Isa. 6:3, Psalm 33:5), nature can reveal God, the Power. Miracles are the greatest power witnessed from behind the veil of physical reality, from the cracks in physical reality. So, here is the point:

> From the breakdown in the realness of the screen of experience of moment-to-moment reality, where the screen of external reality is seen to be just that—a screen that does not represent a 3D reality behind it—and where one knows this vacuousness of the external topological and temporal reality as just the mindscreen (see the next chapter for more clarification), where in that meditation, and in that experience, you choose to have awareness of Christ who is everywhere, to call to Him who is omnipresent, on Him the I AM that I AM who wants to show Himself to you, in this rejection of the world, this ultimate state of anti-evil (see chapter 3), one will directly exist with the Creator, Jesus Christ, the divine Logos, in what could only be the most direct way.

Often Christians state that proof of God exists through the _magnificence of Creation_, where He is seen or known through the natural. But I find this a seriously problematical issue, and I think we can quickly see that this is not at all what is intended by Romans 1:20—where 1:20 may very likely involves the opposite view: that it is seeing _beyond_ nature, to God who is omnipresently _in_ nature but not part of nature (_in but not of_).

Look carefully at Romans 1:20, in the KJV, where we see the following breakdown:

a. Invisible things, including God, are *seen* (this is the theme from of our findings on the definition of faith in 4).

b. But the invisible things that are seen are things have something to do with creation of the world (that is, the invisible things have some involvement with the things of nature that we can see).

c. And the invisible things seen are understood by created things (noneternal things) that we can see: *nature*.

So, indeed, the dominant theme here is that the invisible-eternal entities are understood because of the visible-created entities. This might be understood as the things created—their form and motion, their magnificence and goodness—reveal God, but if one goes that route, we have the difficult situation where we have to explain how the form and nature of *fallen* things reveal the *unfallen* God, how that which is damaged by the scars of sin can reveal the unfathomable transcendent creator-God who is perfect and devoid of any sin or scars of sin.

I think a far safer way to interpret Romans 1:20 is not to hold that the ways of natural things reveal God, since that would be like suggesting that things with the scars of sin point to God, which is a heresy and contradiction. Rather, I think that the way to go is to believe that when a salvific Christian looks into nature, *they will see the Creator <u>beyond</u> nature*, distinct from nature, in-but-not-of nature: nature is only God's tool for breakthrough—that is, for breaking-out of the natural, to experience of God—where breakages in nature, not the forms and structures of nature themselves, to lead to the revelation Romans 1:20 involves. The things of nature, being fallen, cannot contain the picture of God—only by seeing past them, to their eternal Creator beyond them, can thing that are made reveal uncreated God. This second way of interpreting the breakthrough of Romans 1:20 is precisely what nonphysical Calvinism involves.

> The eternal and created (non-eternal) have opposite many properties, so one cannot be seen in the other—that would be like saying we can see squareness in the circle, or circularity in the cube. Romans 1:20 must be talking about breakthrough experience, where by seeing one realm a _breakthrough_ into the other is recieved—but where a _break-through_ is considered a literal breakage: we can't see the invisible-eternal by anything do with what is visible-noneternal (since invisible-eternal is not of the visible-noneternal), but rather by a gap, or absence, or a crack what is beyond, within, and not-identical to the visible eternal.

To believe that the properties of the visible-created-noneternal point to properties they don't have is like saying by looking at the square I gain positive information about the circle see the invisible through the visible for that reason, which is a logical contradiction, since there is no circularity to be extracted from the square. And only a breakable from the concept of squareness can I go to have understanding of circularity. Likewise, I find a more straightforward interpretation of Romans 1:20 to be such that the created things show us the invisible by the gaps in the created things. In simpler words, a disruption in nature, by God, reveals God, and that's what Romans 1:20 means by "being understood by the things that are made".

> _This is why when Jesus was no earth He revealed disruptions in the order of nature (namely miracles) to reveal Himself. Jesus did not point to a tree and say, "don't look at me, look over there at that tree, see how magnificent that tree is, by that you can know me: you must go_

around me, through the tree, to see me, even though I am standing right here in front of you. ."

Rather, Jesus says to keep our eyes on Him, and when we do, what he reveals are gaps in nature (miracles) that show what is beyond (Trinity). And considering this translation of Romans 1:20:

Romans 1:20 English Standard Version (ESV)

20 For his invisible attributes, namely, his eternal power and divine nature, have been clearly perceived, ever since the creation of the world, in the things that have been made. So they are without excuse.

It says *in* the things that have been made, not *of* the things that have been made. That is a key difference. The wood is *in* the flames, but the fire and wood, although a continuous system, are *distinct*, they have different properties, and you can't get from one to the other. To understand each you must understand how they are opposite of each other (flammable vs. flame, one emits light by using the power of the other, one is fueling the other, etc.). If I said the wood is of the flame, it would sound like the wood and fire were more close to being identical, as if I could understand wood by understanding flame. When a salvific Christian looks into nature, they will see the Creator *beyond, past, through, behind nature*: nature is only the tool for breakthrough, and the things have nature, being fallen, cannot contain the picture of God. In more direct terms, nonphysical Calvinism prompts us to see that the physical forms do not have as much real-ness, as much reality, as the evil-oriented worldly mind believes, and the function of the physical forms is *to see past them, to the creator-Logos*. This world is fading away (1 John 2:15-17), but the infinite God behind it is an ever-present all-consuming Fire.

So I will agree with Calvinists that God revealing Himself, as discussed in Roans 1:20, is a key element, but with the variation that God is seen in the _breakage_ of nature, not in the forms and ways of fallen nature itself. In the Gospels, God (Jesus) specifically made Himself known by doing things to break the rules, the laws, of nature—namely perform miracles, which are a _breaking_ of the laws of nature--and thus it was specifically showing a Power outside of nature that the revelation involved.

Maximal Joy

I would assert that the core of Calvinism is about joy. I believe that, for example, Arminianism (often considered to be, in many ways, the other end of the spectrum as Calvinism), and especially Eastern Orthodox Christianity, are absolutely theologies of joy, and can be just as much as Calvinism. But I believe that the amount of _trust_ in God that Calvinism requires, and the consequent requirement of the all-important death of (crucifixion of) the self which is required for maximal trust in Christ, more directly points one right to the joy of the Lord, if, that is, one fully engages the theology of Calvinism[71]. Consider what Forster, who also argues Calvinism is a maximally joyous theology, writes about some of these issues:

> Being a Calvinist means living in the fullness of joy that Peter expresses in [1 Peter 1:3-7], by embracing its full meaning and all the implications of that meaning for doctrine, piety, and life. Defending

[71] Many who call themselves Calvinists actually mix n many non-Calvinist ideas, as is well-known and widely discussed. A great example of this is how many in Calvinist churches is saved because they made a choice, of their own volition to some degree, not 100 percent God's doing, to believe in Christ and therefore or eternally secured (forever saved), but that view is anti-Calvinist, and fully Arminian (see Acts 13:48).

Calvinism means defending that fullness of joy by defending full meaning. (Forster 19)

I believe Calvinism is about going as deeply into Scripture and joy as possible, and that's what nonphysical Calvinism / fullness Calvinism are all about, and in the process of that, the theology deepens, which is much of what is going on in this chapter, along with chapters 6, 8-10 are about.

Nonphysical Calvinism, unlike any other theology I know, has the capacity, in my opinion, and from my experience, to bring a person directly to experience the omnipresent light of God everywhere—what the Eastern Orthodox Christians term the Uncreated Light. The Logos (Jesus Christ) is the Creator of all things (John 1:1-14, Col. 1:16-17, Rev. 4:11), in all things (Isa. 6:3, Eph. 4:6, etc.) He is the source, the Maker of all things at very moment, so we should *expect* that if we can see down to the last bit of the reality of the physical things, we should be able to see the Creator, or at least sense the Creator most deeply (as deeply as He will allow Himself to be revealed), to directly experience Him behind and within the veil of physical reality—behind the screen of the contradictory physical forms. In many ways nonphysical Calvinism is about following the evidence and literally breaking down our mind's confidence in the primacy of physical reality (disintegrating it, is probably a better word), wherein all that is left is God, for those who seek Him with all their hearts (Jer. 29:13). For these reasons, nonphysical Calvinism brings maximal joy, where one needs to make this fullness of a way of life in order to prevent falling away from God.[72]

---

[72] By "falling away from God," I do not mean losing one's salvation, or something like that. I merely mean precisely what is stated in Hebrews 6:4-6.

Predestination

Calvinism involves God having the fullest control over reality, as compared to other theologies, as mentioned above. If total control by God is found in nonphysical Calvinism, then double predestination, the distinctly Calvinist view of predestination, is quite true in nonphysical Calvinism. This is because what the world presented to a person (what is viewed in the mindscreen) is chosen by God, created by God, with only limited influence by free will. For this reason, what is presented to a person in their experience of reality will contain a specific level of revelation, ppop

> Proverbs 16:4 King James Version (KJV)
>
> 4 The Lord hath made all things for himself: yea, even the wicked for the day of evil.
>
> Romans 9:20-24 English Standard Version (ESV)
>
> 20 But who are you, O man, to answer back to God? Will what is molded say to its molder, "Why have you made me like this?" 21 Has the potter no right over the clay, to make out of the same lump one vessel for honorable use and another for dishonorable use? 22 What if God, desiring to show his wrath and to make known his power, has endured with much patience vessels of wrath prepared for destruction, 23 in order to make known the riches of his glory for vessels of mercy, which he has prepared beforehand for glory— 24 even us whom he has called, not from the Jews only but also from the Gentiles?

Nonphysical Calvinism is the Purest Interpretation of the Word of God, Involving the Most Intense Adherence to It

To my knowledge, Calvinism holds, more than other theologies, more to the idea that when the Bible was written, it was God doing the writing. Many theologies hold that humans had a part in the writing, to various degrees, but Calvinism does not: *God is the author* (see Hesselink 2012, 8-9). This would seem to entail, it would seem, a great increasing in the level of trust in the Word, than I see Christians often having. It says in the Word that we should not trust our own understanding, or add and subtract from the Word, but in my opinion, Christians do not self-check if they are doing that quite enough. Perhaps that is why Christians often deemphasize passages that discussing how we are to stop sinning, deny the world, fix our eyes on Jesus, and so forth. This sort of message utterly fills the Bible, but they are either topics that are not talked about much, or when they are, they are usually distorted heavily by Christians, who are often eager to compromise with the world, even if they tell you they do not.

Nonphysical Calvinism theory is of utmost importance in Christian theology, *because it puts maximum de-emphasis on the world*. The world's works are evil (John 7:7), and the world keeps a person from loving the Father (1 John 2:15), so conversely, the greatest amount of closeness go Jesus will keep us a proper distance from the world.

The importance, the status, the value of the world in our minds is a *pinnacle salvation issue*. The world is always a threat, and one which the average Christian in today's world has learned to shrug-off. Nonphysical Calvinism is the maximum, ultimate, *deconstruction*[73] of the world. To have logic lead us, guide us, into having awareness that our lives, our world, everything we see (except God and any inner self-one's own or another's) is—as hinted at in some Scriptures quoted above—like a dream, that all we are seeing is a mindscreen, from my experience, *makes the presence of God burst forth in perhaps the strongest fashion.* When one has arrived at this direct experience of Christ, the other fears and concerns of life fall away, and infinitely joyous communion with God becomes the sole priority. This is very similar to what I call "omnipresence prayer," a topic I gave a sermon on at the jail that I work at earlier in 2018, where it was discussed how God is everywhere, and if we look out at our reality and know that He is everywhere, we develop the capacity *to look past the world*, and become aware of God all around, as if we are experiencing two realties overlapping: our mindscreen experience, which is only inner, and our experience of, awareness of, the omnipresent creator-God, Christ Jesus, the Logos, everywhere (both inner and outer: *omnipresent*).

The world is the source of our problems, we want to transcend it, overcome the world (John 16:33), but if we understand that the world is no more than mindscreen experience, then we can put the troublesome world in its proper level of importance—namely as not so important to obsess over it, and to be in pain over the world due to constant fear and desire about the matters and the things of the world. Nonphysical Calvinism blocks the domination of the

---

[73] I have deliberately chosen this word, which has affinities with postmodern philosophy. Deconstructionism in postmodern philosophy, aimed not the text by at the metaphysics of external reality, at the social world, at science, and anything else exterior to the inner self/mind, is in many ways what simulation theory is about—at least in my presentation of Christian theology as simulation theory. I plan to write in the future about how postmodern philosophy is a greater friend to Christianity than I believe most imagine.

world by holding the person in constant awareness that the world is merely a screen, and by that God is felt all around.

The Bible teaches detachment from the world by not looking at the world, but looking at Christ ("fix your eyes on Jesus"), and nonphysical Calvinism obliterates our confidence in the world, so we can let go of the world, of our lives, detach and be citizens of heaven (Phil. 3:20), *right now*. The world is the problem, love the world and we are enemies of the Father. The average Christian does not really want to surrender the world away, detach from world, fully absorb into God and be an enemy of the world and its works of evil (John 7:7).

With nonphysical Calvinist meditation and prayer, we see that the world is just a screen, and by that detachment of the things that are fading away (1 John 2:17), God shows Himself omnipresently. In Scripture, we are told, 'seek the Lord's face," "keep your eyes in Heaven," "fix your eyes on Jesus," and so forth. Nonphysical Calvinist meditation and prayer automatically allows God to pull our eyes to Him continually.

The self is the disease (1 Kings 8:38), and the self has its strength in the world-identification, world-alignment. This is addiction and death. Nonphysical Calvinist theology brings us into hyper-focused presence of God, unconcern with world, and detachment from worldly concerns.

> 2 Corinthians 5:8 King James Version (KJV)
>
> 8 We are confident, I say, and willing rather to be absent from the body, and to be present with the Lord.

> Galatians 5:25 King James Version (KJV)

25 If we live in the Spirit, let us also walk in the Spirit.

Work Cited

Forster, Greg, 2012, _The Joy of Calvinism_, Wheaton, IL: Crossway.

Grupp, Jeff, 2018a, Dec. 31, _Fullness Calvinism: Expanding Calvinist Theology to Resolve Big Theological Puzzles_ [Video File]. YouTube.com, https://www.youtube.com/watch?v=-LhIi8ZhjWM.

Grupp, Jeff, 2018b, "God's Pre-Election Knowledge of the Soul: A New Interpretation of Biblical Election and Predestination Showing Why God Only Chose Some Rather Than All," in _Theologic: Revelation, Calvinism, Surrender, Nothingness_, Kalamazoo: Praise and Love Church, (print copy available from Lulu books), pages 5-33.

Hesselink, John I, "The Revelation of God in Creation and Scripture: Calvin's Theology and Its Early Reception," in Billings, Todd J., and Hesselink, John I (Editors), 2012, _Calvin's Theology and Its Reception: Disputes, Developments, and New Possibilities_, Louisville: Westminster John Knox Press, pages 3-24.

10. Nonphysical Calvinism: Mindscreen Implantation and Experiencing God

Psalm 90:3-6 English Standard Version (ESV)

3 You return man to dust and say, "Return, O children of man!" 4 For a thousand years in your sight are but as yesterday when it is past, or as a watch in the night. 5 You sweep them away as with a flood; they are like a dream, like grass that is renewed in the morning: 6 in the morning it flourishes and is renewed; in the evening it fades and withers.

Psalm 126:1-3 New International Version (NIV)

1 When the Lord restored the fortunes of Zion, we were like those who dreamed. 2 Our mouths were filled with laughter, our tongues with songs of joy. Then it was said among the nations, "The Lord has done great things for them." 3 The Lord has done great things for us, and we are filled with joy.

Colossians 1:16-17 (NRSV)

16 for in him all things in heaven and on earth were created, things visible and invisible, whether thrones or dominions or rulers or powers—all things have been created through him and for him. 17 He himself is before all things, and in him all things hold together.

Introduction: _God-Faith_, the Most Direct Experience of God

In many ways, this Chapter is a continuation of Chapter 7, in laying-out more of the metaphysics of nonphysical Calvinism, but this chapter mixes that study more with the previous nine chapters, and more with discussion of the prayerful way of life that God-faith involves. Nonphysical Calvinism is the Biblical theology and life-of-prayer that is associated with the most direct experience of God, an experience which I will hereafter call _God-faith._ God-faith also directly reveals to the worshipper of Christ that reality (1) is the hyper-real omnipresent light of Christ (God), and (2) that the experience of physical reality is some sort of computer simulation-like mind-implantation, rather than a realist external reality[74], as discussed in the introduction to Part 3. So the _actual_ realty all around is that of the light from the face of omnipresent creator, Christ Jesus (not the realist external 3D reality), which is seen when our eyes are fully opened—we see in a larger way than normal. The Bible is clear that the actual reality that we are intended to experience is the omnipresent light off emanating from the face of Christ-Logos, which is the experience and way-of-being that I call _God-faith_:

> Psalm 80:19 New American Standard Bible (NASB)
>
> O Lord God of hosts, restore us;
>
> Cause Your face to shine upon us, and we will be saved.

---

[74] I will define "realism" in more detail below, but for now, one can think of it as the belief that the physical world one sees all around them, external to them, is a real 3D external reality outside of them that roughly is as it appears.

Psalm 4:6 New International Version (NIV)

Let the light of your face shine on us.

Psalm 105:4 New American Standard Bible (NASB)

Seek His face continually.

Numbers 6:25-26 New American Standard Bible (NASB)

The Lord make His face shine on you... The Lord lift up His countenance on you...

Matthew 17:2-3 New International Version (NIV)

2 There he was transfigured before them. His face shone like the sun, and his clothes became as white as the light. 3 Just then there appeared before them Moses and Elijah, talking with Jesus.

Directly seeking God's light and face as the function of the Christian daily life (God-faith) is a *pinnacle theme* in the Bible, which we should see everywhere in the world that we look:

John 8:12 English Standard Version (ESV)

12 Again Jesus spoke to them, saying, "I am the light of the world. Whoever follows me will not walk in darkness, but will have the light of life."

Psalm 27:1 English Standard Version (ESV)

27 The Lord is my light and my salvation; whom shall I fear? The Lord is the stronghold of my life; of whom shall I be afraid?

We should expect to see the radiance of God, like rays of sunlight (Matt. 17:2-3, Mal. 4:2), in everything. Consider the following important verse, in two translations:

Hebrews 1:3 English Standard Version (ESV)

3 He is the radiance of the glory of God and the exact imprint of his nature, and he upholds the universe by the word of his power. After making purification for sins, he sat down at the right hand of the Majesty on high,

Hebrews 1:3 New International Version (NIV)

3 The Son is the radiance of God's glory and the exact representation of his being, sustaining all things by his powerful word. After he had provided purification for sins, he sat down at the right hand of the Majesty in heaven.

This dominant theme, coming literally from our Creator, can only be of utter realness, the most serious words of good news we will ever hear:

1 John 1:7 New King James Version (NKJV)

7 But if we walk in the light as He is in the light, we have fellowship with one another, and the blood of Jesus Christ His Son cleanses us from all sin.

God-faith is seeing the light of God's face filling the earth (Isaiah 6:3), omnipresence prayer is the tool for this revelation in Christ, and nonphysical Calvinism is the Biblical metaphysics and model of reality that emerges from this way of direct experiencing of God. We have yet to see Him as He is (1 John 3:2), but God-faith allows us a great taste and awareness of what is to come. Faith is a free gift we receive from the Trinity. In a state of active faith, we know God, and not in that state we are of sin (Romans 14:23), and of the devil (1 John 3:8). The act of faith is to be experiencing god and God doing works in us accordingly (John 14:10).

This chapter shows the more monastic and meditative nature that Christianity was meant to comprise, as is obvious from the Word of God, but which has been largely not taken seriously or ignored. We are commanded to pray always: "Fix your eyes on Jesus…" in Hebrews 12:2 is not a request, it is given as a command, and not following a command of God's is sin (recall our definition of evil: the mind not fixing eyes on the Lord). Here I don't mean that Christianity is to be monastic in the sense of shutting away from the world and not serving the poor, as monasticism is often (and wrongly) associated with today. But rather, I mean the word "monastic" to mean that Christianity is intended to be an around-the-clock prayer vigil, which is, quite obviously, and without a doubt, precisely what the Bible is about, verse after verse, and hence the reason I defined faith as such in Chapter 5 above.

Psalm 73:23-25 English Standard Version (ESV)

23 Nevertheless, I am continually with you; you hold my right hand.

24 You guide me with your counsel, and afterward you will receive me to glory.

25 Whom have I in heaven but you? And there is nothing on earth that I desire besides you.

Hebrews 11:6 New International Reader's Version (NIRV)

6 Without faith it is impossible to please God. Those who come to God must believe that he exists. And they must believe that he rewards those who look to him.

Omnipresence Prayer: The Most Strictly Biblical Mode of Prayer

Omnipresence is one of the attributes of God. Omnipresence prayer is type of prayer that would appear to be most closely in-line with the Bible, and also the way of prayer that leads to the joyful, heavenly realization of nonphysical Calvinist metaphysics. Introduced in the introduction to Part 3 above, omnipresence prayer is a simple prayerfulness that reveals the nonphysical Calvinist ontology of our reality, which, Biblically speaking, is seemingly what prayer is supposed to be like, for the following reasons. If we are contacting, reaching out to, seeking, and looking at God when we are praying and talking to Him, then we will be aware of Him where He *is at*, which is omnipresently all around. If I am talking to *you*, I would need to be *aware* of you, and therefore aware of *where* you *are*, when I am talking directly to you. So wouldn't I have to do the very same when I am talking with God, who is omnipresent? If I do not, wouldn't it be the case that I was actually *not* talking to God, but rather, that I was merely mumbling to myself? If the answer to that (rather obvious) question is yes, then omnipresence prayer becomes the most important issue in any person's life on earth! And it reveals that many people could be praying without really talking *to God*—but rather they are just mumbling to themselves.

On March 17, 2019, I gave a sermon on omnipresence prayer,[75] which follows Isaiah 6:3 and the many other verses in the Bible about omnipresence. Here is an excerpt from the sermon:

> Of all the things the angels could say [while singing in God's temple in Heaven], they mention that the whole earth *is full of the glory of God...* Of all the things they could be concerned with, they are concerned with how the *earth* is full glory of God. Now the glory is typically His face [fn, from Nazarene work], or the light coming off of His face... So His face, the purest essence of God, the epitome of His holiness, fills *the earth*, [what you see all around you]. And what happens to Isaiah when he sees this? He's ruined, he's broken. He's not lifted up to experience some sort of spiritual catapult—no, he's *broken*... he is nothing... So, God is at every place of the existence of any reality. At every point in space as you look out into this room, Jesus is here, in His fullness— not partially... His *all* is at every point in space, and filling the entire room... God fills every point in space... God is in His fullness in this room *now*. He is also in Heaven, but He's also *here now*. There is an everywhere-ness to God... If you look out at this room, you should be

---

75 Grupp, Jeff, 2019, March 17, God IS EVERYWHERE, Sermon, Pastor Jeff Grupp, 3-17-19, [Video File]. YouTube.com Channel: Praise and Love, URL: https://www.youtube.com/watch?v=PXXKEXg--XA.

seeing God *first*. Seeing Him with your heart... your mind's eye, your mind's feelings, your mind's *awareness*. There should be a *knowing*: you *know* He's *here*, in this room. You see matter, but coinciding with it is the power of God, His fullness. This is the *answer*. This is your *healing*. He's also in Heaven above, but [in addition] He's *here now*... The attribute of omnipresence is really our way of getting *connected* to God, experiencing Him, more than anything else. He's *right here*: all around you and inside you... I think people are afraid of the explosion of joy that omnipresence involves. (Grupp 2019)

You can go and listen to the rest of the sermon as needed to here more details, but that is a basic introduction to omnipresence prayer. Biblically speaking, omnipresence prayer should be the around-the-clock awareness, pointedness, concentration, and meditation of one's life. Everywhere you can look, right now, in your reality, God fully fills every point, every region, every speck, every huge region, you only need to be *aware* of this—to make the decision that you believe, and *know*, this—and you will have awareness of Him everywhere.[76]

Mindscreen, Nothingness, and the God's Creation of Evil

As mentioned above, and as has been well discussed by Reformed theologians, sin can be viewed as *nothingness* (see and Krotke 2005, Grupp 2018d). The experience of physical reality (rather than God-faith), the contradiction of matter, accompanies nothingness, in the dreariness of the

---

[76] As discussed in Chapter 5, much of what faith is, is belief, but it grows and develops into direct communion with God. The reader is advised to see Grupp 2018c for more information.

life of non-faith (Romans 14:23), of not looking at the Lord from moment-to-moment, living in the inner production of evil.

Contradictory items are ubiquitously believed in professional philosophy to not exist, and cannot even be imagined (try to picture a round square in your mind). God-faith reveals what is fully real: awareness of the omnipresent light from Christ's face, filling all of reality, in every direction that one can look. The mindscreen entities are experienced as less real—and only as real as being the mostly meaningless (Eccl. 1:2), banal objects of the picture-screen of the vessel that is doing evil. Mindscreen elements, made of contradiction, should not exist, and being composed of contradiction, only give rise to nothingness when we exist gazing at the mindscreen elements, rather than resting in the infinite gaze of God-faith. And that we can *even "see"* the contradictory cinema of physical reality in our mindscreens, and that the contradictory *can even* "exist" in the mindscreen, is only due to the supernatural all-powerful creator-Spirit (YHVH) implanting those impossible items into the human consciousness. This is the creation of evil by God: the looking at the physical existence (the mindscreen), generating moment-to-moment nothingness.

> *This is how God creates evil (Isaiah 45:7 KJV), as discussed in Chapter 3: via the creation and allowing of the free will mind to look at the inner mindscreen (experience of the physical world) that God implants, sustaining the mind as it does, generating the inner production of evil, wherein that free will creates nothingness (sin).*

That is the most precise definition of evil, God's creation of it, and how humans create sin from it. *Evil is not a force in the world, it is a perspective in the mind.*

God-faith, the act of _meditation on Christ_, the act of moving awareness from evil and nothingness to the omnipresent One. We found in Chapter 5, Biblically speaking, that the ever-present, moment-to-moment communion with the Spirit of God, is the around-the-clock antidote to inner evil.

2 Corinthians 10:5 New International Version (NIV)

5 We demolish arguments and every pretension that sets itself up against the knowledge of God, and we take captive every thought to make it obedient to Christ.

Something like a complete break from physical reality is what the Bible instructs. I understand how the typical Christian will not be yearning for this level of intensity, but I am only wanting to adhere to what God has spoken, and His message is clear:

James 4:4 King James Version (KJV)

4 ...know ye not that the friendship of the world is enmity with God? whosoever therefore will be a friend of the world is the enemy of God.

1 John 2:15 New King James Version (NKJV)

15 Do not love the world or the things in the world. If anyone loves the world, the love of the Father is not in him.

Nonphyscal Mindscreen

The Bible says God is everywhere, God fills all things (Num. 14:21, Jer. 23:24), and all things are in God (Col. 1:16-17). Human minds are in Christ (2 Cor. 5:17, Col. 2:10, Gal. 3:28, Rom. 8:1), and Christ is in human minds (Gal. 2:20, Col. 3:11, 1 Cor. 6:19), and the Kingdom of God is within the human created being (Luke 17:21). Consider John 15:5:

> I am the vine, ye are the branches: He that abideth in me, and I in him, the same bringeth forth much fruit: for without me ye can do nothing. (KJV)

Colossians 3:11 even goes as far as to say Christ is all, reflecting Philippians 2:5: we are to be the mind of Christ. The physical reality is a problem, or an enemy to the created human being (James 4:4, 1 John 2:15), and to being in a life of faith-awareness in God's presence (Ps. 16:11), and to the created being residing in Heaven (Phil. 3:20), now (Ps. 13:5 NIV, Gal. 2:20).

The picture we have from Christian theology is that all is in the Holy Spirit, and Spirit is in all (Col. 3:11). All exists within the Christian God (nonphysical), and thus all is nonphysical, as is expected with the mindscreen metaphysics, but not with realist representationalist philosophy.

> This all leads to a question:

> *How can we all be in a nonphysical Spirit if we are physical? How does the physical fit into the nonphysical? How can the nonspatial fit into the spatial (which is impossible)?*

If God is nonphysical, and all exists within Him, it would seem a sounder theology to hold that we are nonphysical spirits that exist in Him, and that we exist in God's created evil (existing in free-willed selfhood witnessing the mindscreen), rather than suggesting that physical hunks of contradictory matter exist in an all-powerful nonphysical perfect creator-Spirit.

The Bible never mentions that externality is real—that realism is true—and on the other hand, there is tremendous confusion in the Bible on spatial mechanics: the Kingdom of God is inside of us? All things are in Christ? And at the same time, Christ is all and in all? If one hopes to make any sense of these topologically confused matters, one has to toss-aside ordinary three- and four-dimensional spacetime. But if we do that, we go directly to nonphysical Calvinism.

The Simulation Theory Argument

If mindscreen experience is actually some sort of mindscreen implantation by God, much like a self-aware, conscious computer simulation, rather than an externality experiencing mind-in-a-body that has its experience by interacting with a 3D physical external world all around (the realist scenario), then it might be demonstrable that the physical reality cannot be _represented_ in a brain or nervous system, and for that reason, a human mindscreen cannot experience physical reality as typically believed, which is as a physical body correctly consciously experiencing via internal picture-screen consciousness recreations and maps of externality through a nervous system. Rather, mindscreen experience would not be generated by apprehending and processing information from an exteriority, from the world, but rather via from some other source, but made to _appear_ to be about exteriority. In other words, humans view physical reality as a cinematic-like screen (mindscreen), but where the pixelated digital pictures, and screen-imagery, of landscapes and realities that comprise their mindscreen consciousnesses, but they also contain olfactory, auditory, gustatory, and tactile elements, in addition to visual (picture screen) consciousness, that *do not exist in brain-meat* (that is, if you look inside a person's brain during surgery, you only see neuronal tissues, not televisual screens, sound-speakers, and so forth). According to the idea that mindscreen information is created by God, implanted into the human vessel for experiencing, the brain is just another theme of the mindscreen's implanted mind-dependent reality, not a real mind-independent item: the brain, like a tree or a cloud, is just another part of the story of the cinematic nonrepresentationalist mindscreen existence.

The following argument[77] shows the tremendous difficulty of formulating mindscreen experience as having anything to do with physical brain-meat (in addition to all difficulties demonstrated in the chapters prior to this one):

1. Human experiencing contains *picture imagery* in subjective experiencing (ordinary consciousness involves picture consciousness: a picture screen—a mindscreen—in experience).

2. If consciousness (mindscreen) is a physical process, then it experiences and interacts with physical reality through matter (brain, nervous system), but matter, such as brains (lobes, tissues, neurons, chemicals, molecules, cerebrospinal fluid, etc.), does not have advanced feeling-infused televisual picture-screens of self-awareness any sort inside of them.

---

[77] This argument is given in terms of sight experience, but can be given in terms of other mental intensities (auditory, gustatory, olfactory, and tactile experiences, in addition to other intensities not as widely discussed, such as the "feelings" one has of ascending or descending, such as in an elevator).

3. Organic brain matter, which is _meat_, does not seem like the sort of medium that can have precise and vivid mindscreen digitation in it (feeling, incredibly organized and patterned picture thoughts, etc.), and suggesting brain cells or groups of cells do, would be analogous to suggesting that a hunk of meat can have an ultra-advanced self-aware cinematic mindscreen in it that has emotion, feeling, self-awareness, color experiencing, problem solving, and, possibly, qualia and free will. In other words, to suggest that meat can have in it, or could function as, self-aware feeling-infused digital picture screen televisions, would be to suggest that inside of meat are seemingly supernatural, or at least ineffable, computers of such complexity that humans cannot even define them yet. In this chapter, the thesis will be taken that such is impossible, and meat does not have such self-aware televisions, let alone _experienced_ televisual screens of any sort.[78]

4. Mindscreen experience not only involves the cinematic feeling-content of mind, but also _experiencing_, which is a self-aware "entity," for lack of more precise wording, and which, it is safe to say is, to this point, ineffable, and a process that is beyond scientific measurement. It is seemingly safe to conclude that feeling-infused cinematic self-_awareness_ is not derivable from chemicals: it appears safe to conclude that no matter how many chemicals one puts in a vat, and which way one mixes them in any complicated way, the chemistry will not start _feeling_, will not spontaneously come to _self-awareness_ and picture-screen cinematics. I can imprint or cause an image in a chemical soup, such as by cymatics

---

[78] Jack Gallant's research at UC Berkley, which might, at this point, be considered by some to contain an objection to this premise, and thus to this argument overall, will be discussed in detail below, and will be found to not contain any such objection.

(sound vibrations), but the chemistry will not have experiencing, it seems safe to assume, since, no such instance of self-aware, feeling-infused experiencing chemicals have ever been observed or created, including in the chemical soup of the human brain. If we can assume chemicals are not the sort of entity that can serve as a medium for such experiencing, then a physical brain cannot consciously be an *experiencing* mindscreen.

5. Following points 3 and 4, picture consciousness is not located within, and does not come from, organic matter, so picture consciousness (or any other ineffable intensities of mind) cannot operate via brain (or matter) to interact with and/or perceive and represent physical reality or any exteriority.

6. The human mind (mindscreen) cannot be located within the physical reality (in the physical-empirical cosmos), as an organic being that it believes it is located within from the indications of the mindscreen.

7. Human mindscreen experience of physical reality is not the reality that the mindscreen exists amid.

8. Human mindscreen experience of physical reality does not represent mind-independent physical objects and a mind-independent externality.

9. CONCLUSION: Nonrepresentational mental experiencing of a physical reality is a fabricated (artificial) mental model (simulation) since it is not caused by any externality.

A human believes he has a mind for interacting with the external world via organic matter (a brain or nervous system), but the argument just given shows that a mind does not, and cannot, use organic matter, or any known matter or medium, to perceive and represent an external. A human is *not* where he assumes he is (in the physical reality), and his interaction with physical reality is some sort of internal cinema, rather than light-information taken-in, obtained, perceived, from an externality outside of the mindscreen, as the realist scenario. A human mindscreen beholds a colorful array of picture imagery in orderly sequence, and thus the cinematic mindscreen is known to exist directly (nonrepresentationally), but contents represented beyond the mindscreen cannot be known directly.[79] Brain-meat is not the sort of medium _needed_ to create ineffable self-aware representational feeling-consciousness, our bodies cannot produce world-experience, and brain-meat therefore is merely part of the simulation reality. In more precise words, if, in the represented world (which is the simulation, according to this book), there is no actual screen known to exist, no self-aware digital cinema-screen measured to be _experiencing_ or _experienced_, as premises 3 and 4 of the simulation theory argument above would appear to indicate, then representational picture-screen consciousness of a world outside of itself, cannot exist via the physical world that the mindscreen involves.

In addition to imagistic mental screens, human consciousness also involves olfactory, gustatory, auditory, and tactile experiences, just as mental picture screens are in brains via representation, brains and matter also do not contain vibrating speakers or hearing devices, nor taste buds to taste, or noses for smelling. _Experiencing_ of external reality (that is believe to exist) does not occur in the noses, eyes, ears, tongues, and skin sensors. It occurs in mental space, where the precise nature or location of mentation has not been discovered. In other words, the self-aware _experiencing_ of these mental realities has not been measured in brain-meat. I can put in my inner

---

[79] According to the standard representationalist model, the inner screen is directly perceived, the external world is not directly perceived.

experience, right now, the sound of a car horn that I heard earlier today, but there is no vibration and sound system in my brain, so the sound experience occurs by an a means foreign to what sound *is*, which is matter vibration.

As we discussed in Chapter 1, ubiquitously, it is assumed by academics that mind is (somehow) physical, despite the lack of evidence or even counter-evidence. This is where virtually all academic work on consciousness begins, and to suggest otherwise is nearly an embarrassment. Direct awareness of mindscreen consciousness reveals that it appears not physical, but that finding is not tolerated by contemporary academics, despite the direct (introspective) evidence, which, it seems, could be widely agreed upon. Consider what Searle writes, in the appropriately titled *The Mystery of Consciousness*, in the third paragraph of the book:

> Compared to mountains and molecules, consciousness seems "mysterious," "ethereal," even "mystical." Consciousness does not seem to be "physical" in the way that other features of the brain, such as neuron firings, are physical. Nor does it seem to be reducible to physical processes by the usual sorts of scientific analyses that have worked for such physical properties such as heat and solidity.[80]

But then, in the next paragraph of his book, and believing the only way to handle the seeming nonphysicality of consciousness, is via dualism, rather than simulation theory, or something like nonphysical Calvinism, Searle writes:

> But dualism as traditionally conceived seems a hopeless theory because, having made a strict distinction between the mental and the

---

[80] Searle, John, 1977, *The Mystery of Consciousness*, New York: New York Review of Books, p. xii.

physical world, it cannot then make the relation of the two intelligible. It seems that to accept dualism is to give up the entire scientific worldview that we have spent nearly four centuries to attain. So, what are we to do?[81]

Note that Searle starts with the *assumption* that matter and contradictory physical objects of the world outside of him are real, and then states that a nonmaterial mind cannot exist since it cannot interrelate with the material world. But if we merely abandon the unverified assumption that matter and the contradictory outside world are real entities independent of mind, then Searle's assumption fails, and the following argument emerges:

> Since mind is, as Searle notes, seemingly nonphysical, and since the external world cannot be verified to exist independently of mindscreen experience, we can infer that, since nonphysical mind and physical world seemingly cannot interact then the physical world is not real (not a mind-independent realist externality), but is only a mindscreen reality.

Searle's account is an example of the way it is assumed that mind can only exist via brain, which, appears, however, to be incorrect, given the simulation theory argument above. Searle glues onto the idea that brains (meat) must have consciousness (mindscreens). In other words, instead of following a coherent and evidence-based theory (that mind might be more like a nonphysical item, so evidence of the existence of the world is assumption at best and contradiction at worst), he locks onto a perhaps impossible thesis (mind is physical, so world is real and meat has computers and screens inside of it of vast, even seemingly near supernatural complexity). This is

---

[81] Ibid., pp. xii-xiii.

why something like the simulation theory argument, even though most logical, is not even approached by professional academics, who, rather, start with the aforementioned assumption that supernatural televisions and computer programs spontaneously evolved in, and exist within, brain meat, even though no such televisions and computers have been discovered in any single piece of meat (such as the brain) yet.

Mind-body dualism vanishes with simulation theory. Reality is neither considered to be materialist, idealist, or a combination of the two. Those are considered ideas in the mindscreen simulation, and instead, reality is known to be merely (1) mindscreen experience on the one hand, and (2) desimulated experience of the creator-simulator on the other. The thought of abandoning the physicalist thesis is nearly unthinkable in our current climate of academic materialism in the contemporary world. But this is strange, given the well-known power of the discoveries of Kant and those after him: that our reality is our experience, and we are locked inside of it, wherein, all we ever know is experience (mindscreen), and whether anything else exists is assumption. In other words, matter, the physical world, and ideas of physicalism, are all part of experience (mindscreen), and professional academics who hold to physicalism merely have to make a first, non-Kantian assumption, that physical reality is real and that our representations are about a reality outside of our self that is real. And as is also well-known, this is a gargantuan assumption! I merely don't make this assumption, and the simple conclusion then that one arrives at is, quite plainly, *simulation theory*.

Another almost even more troubling reason that the physicalist-realist assumption is plainly incorrect, is the seeming fact that physical reality involves contradiction, to the point that all aspects of physical reality reduce to contradiction. This was the finding of Zeno in his Paradoxes. I also discussed this at great length in several publications (see Grupp 2005-2006 in Works Cited), especially my article on mereological nihilism (Grupp 2006a), which went far beyond mere Zenoic discussion of the contradiction of physical reality via the Measure Paradox, and my 2013 talk on simulation theory at the University of Michigan – Dearborn. For over 2500 years, the way intellectuals have dealt with these well-known contradictions in physical reality, is to merely ignore them, and assert that there must be an explanation, which we humans just don't know yet. This is a problematical and concerning move, especially in light of the fact that the aforementioned contradictions of physical reality cease to be a problem in simulation theory. Intellectuals, therefore, go even to nonlogical measures to attempt to adhere to the physicality of the mindscreen presentation, and to keep their faith in the realness of externality, they behold from moment-to-moment of their mental life, despite the many obvious and insurmountable contradictions found in the simple descriptions of physical reality, via realism[82] (R), that philosophers have been struggling with (or bypassing) for over 2000 years (such as dualism, physicalism of mind, representationalism and the homunculus problem, Zeno's paradoxes, mereological nihilism, and so on).

Objection to the Simulation Theory Argument: Jack Gallant's Research

---

[82] Hereafter, define *realism* (R) as follows: Representationalism, and the idea that there is a physical reality outside of the mindscreen that is not only real outside of the representations, but where the inner representations more-or-less accurately map the externality. In other words, realism is the trust and belief that what is experienced about the world in the mind is how the external world actually is. When a person sees a tree, the inner mental picture of the tree is merely a picture of a real mind-independent entity in a physical world. In professional philosophy, this is also often called naïve realism, or direct realism

Consider this passage from an article:

Scientists at the University of California, Berkeley, have managed to decode and reconstruct dynamic visual experiences processed by the human brain. Currently, researchers are only able to reconstruct movie clips people have already viewed. However, the breakthrough is expected to pave the way for reproducing the movies inside our heads that no one else sees - such as dreams and memories.

"This is a major leap toward reconstructing internal imagery," explained Professor Jack Gallant, a UC Berkeley neuroscientist and coauthor of the study published online today in the journal *Current Biology*. "We are opening a window into the movies in our minds." According to Gallant, practical applications of the technology could eventually include a better understanding of what is happening in the minds of those who cannot communicate verbally, such as stroke victims, coma patients and individuals with neurodegenerative diseases. It may also lay the groundwork for brain-machine interface so that people with cerebral palsy or paralysis can guide computers with their minds...

"Our natural visual experience is like watching a movie," said Shinji Nishimoto, lead author of the study and a post-doctoral researcher in Gallant's lab. "In order for this technology to have wide applicability, we must understand how the brain processes these dynamic visual experiences"... They watched two separate sets of Hollywood movie trailers, while an fMRI measured blood flow through the visual cortex, the part of the brain that processes visual information. On the computer, the brain was divided into small, three-dimensional cubes known as volumetric pixels, or "voxels." The brain activity was recorded while subjects viewed the first set of clips which were fed into a computer program that learned, second by second, to associate visual patterns in the movie with the corresponding brain activity. Brain activity evoked by the second set of clips was used to test the movie reconstruction algorithm. This was done by feeding 18 million seconds of random YouTube videos into the computer program so it could predict the brain activity each film clip would most likely evoke in each subject. Finally, the 100 clips that the computer program determined were most similar to the clip that the subject had probably seen were merged to produce a blurry, yet continuous reconstruction of the original movie. Reconstructing movies using brain scans has been somewhat of a challenge because the blood flow signals measured using fMRI change much more slowly than the neural signals that encode dynamic information in movies. As such, most previous attempts to decode brain activity tended to focus on static images.

"We addressed this problem by developing a two-stage model that separately describes the underlying neural population and blood flow signals," Nishimoto added.

Ultimately, Nishimoto said, scientists want to understand how the brain processes dynamic visual events that are experienced in everyday life.

"We need to know how the brain works in naturalistic conditions... For that, we need to first understand how the brain works while we are watching movies."[83]

---

[83] Brain imaging reveals the movies in our minds," September 22, 2011, by Trent Nouveau, *TG Daily*, http://www.tgdaily.com/general-sciences-features/58630-brain-imaging-reveals-the-movies-in-our-minds.

It should be somewhat expected that the PVC (Primary Visual Cortex) would be discovered to have patterning correlating to vision experience, since, for example, such replicating of light information imprints starts in the eyes, where the imprint of what light brings through the eyes forms a picture and template of how light impacted the eyes. So, to see this transferred information to the PVC should be expected.

Gallant's research is related to another important question:

> if mind transcends brain, and/or is not equal to an aspect of the brain, then why do brain damage victims experience mind changes in predictable ways based on the brain damage, as if brain malfunctioning predictably distorts mind?

The correlations are not always straightforward, however (example given below). But putting that aside in order to discuss this matter, this point leads to another question: *What if mind uses brain, as it's "computer", so to speak, to manage the human body, to varying degrees?* Wouldn't we expect brain and mind to show such correlations, if the two work in a tight relationship? If the engine does not work, the wheels won't move. If the engine works, the wheels will move. If the engine works partially, wouldn't the wheels move in a corresponding way, with as much capacity as the engine gives? Why would we expect different and/or nonsynchronous correlations from the mind-brain system? The idea that brain damage shows how mind is physical, and is only part of the brain, is a short-sighted conclusion.

Back to Gallant's research, what the simulation argument above says is, essentially, that we can't have an ultra-advanced television made out of meat, but Gallant is, essentially, saying, despite how difficult it is to believe that brain-meat can have televisual data inside of it, and that meat can function as televisual data, we have discovered the rudiments of this brain-meat television. In other words, essentially, the simulation argument shows a paradox about experiencing the world via meat (brains), and Gallant's research purports so show that, surprisingly, there is no paradox, we just had not discovered it yet.

So, which view is correct? The simulation argument above, or Gallant's findings? If we find a clear and powerful contradiction in physical reality surrounding the concept that brains can take-in light-information via the eyes to form neural patterns in the PVC, then the idea that Gallant's research provides a problem for premise 3 of the simulation argument would fail, and the simulation theory argument would be the stronger thesis. It would then follow that Gallant's research is just an aspect of our computer programmed simulated existence, rather than a problem for the simulation theory argument.

And there *is* such a contradiction found in physical reality. Consider this account of the discovery of a person that could think, and who was even an honor's student in mathematics, but who had nearly no brain, published in the journal *Science*:

> Lorber believe that his observations on a series of hydrocephalics who have severely reduced brain tissue throws into question many traditional notions about the brain… "There's a young student at this university," says Lorber, "who has an IQ of 126, has gained a first-class honors degree in mathematics, and is socially completely normal. And yet the boy has virtually no brain." The student's physician at the university noticed that the youth had a slightly larger than normal head, and so referred him to Lorber, simply out of interest. "When we did a

brain scan on him," Lorber recalls, "we saw that instead of the normal 4.5-centimeter thickness of brain tissue between the ventricles and the cortical surface, there was just a thin layer of mantle measuring a millimeter or so. His cranium is filled mainly with cerebrospinal fluid...

But, startling as it may seem, this case is nothing new to the medical world. "Scores of similar accounts litter the medical literature, and they go back a long way," observes Patrick Wall, professor of anatomy at University College, London... How can someone with a grossly reduced cerebral mantle not only move among his fellows with no apparently social deficit, but also reach high academic achievement? How is it that in some hydrocephalics whose brains are severely distorted asymmetrically, the expected one-sided paralysis is typically absent? ... It is... not surprising that many hydrocephalics suffer intellectual and physical disabilities. What is surprising, however, is that a substantial proportion of patients appear to escape functional impairment in spite of grossly abnormal brain structure.[84,]

---

[84] "Is Your Brain Really Necessary?" *Science*. 1980. Vol 210. 12. December. P. 1232-1234.
Also, and perhaps related to this issue, box jellyfish have eyes (24 of them) but no brain, so how does it process information from the eyes? how does it make 'decisions' about it's reality (since, presumably, eyes prompt such activity as making decisions) from the eye info without a brain? Where does the information from the eyes go if there is no brain? See Brainless Jellyfish Navigates with Specialized Eyes, by Wynne Perry, *LiveScience*, 4/28/2011, http://www.livescience.com/13929-box-jellyfish-eyes-navigation-brain.html, where we find this passage:

> The skyward gaze of one set of eyes belonging to box jellyfish provides evidence that these creatures -- which lack a conventional brain -- are capable of sophisticated behavior. New research has shown that one species of jellyfish uses one set of eyes to navigate and keep itself close to home.
> "It is a surprise that a jellyfish -- an animal normally considered to be lacking both brain and advanced behavior -- is able to perform visually guided navigation, which is not a trivial behavioral task," said lead researcher Anders Garm of the University of Copenhagen. "This shows that the behavioral abilities of simple animals, like jellyfish, may be underestimated." Box jellyfish have 24 eyes of four different types, and two of them -- the upper and lower lens eyes -- *can form images and resemble the eyes of vertebrates like humans*. The other eyes are more primitive. It was already known that box jellyfish's vision allows them to perform simpler tasks, like responding to light and avoiding obstacles. (Itals added.)

There are many cases of hydrocephalics with shockingly little brain matter. My point here won't be to try to say that brain matter is not being used, but my point will be, rather, to suggest that we do not have evidence that there is a PVC at work in situations like with Lorber's honors student in mathematics. In other words, if there are cases where honors students in mathematics use nearly zero, or perhaps zero brain matter, to have visual experience of the world, with no evidence of a PVC at work in this representing process, and evidence that a PVC does not even exist in this particular person, then we arrive at the following _reductio ad absurdum_ argument to the idea that our reality involves humans who have brains that create televisual picture-screen experience:

1. Gallant's research of brain-meat having televisual picture-screen representations in the neural activity provides a conceivable contradiction to premise 3 of the simulation theory argument, wherein the simulation theory argument would possibly fail.

2. Lorber (and others) have shown that some hydrocephalics function normally or even above normally without having primary visual cortex brain matter, as far as anyone can tell, or much of any brain matter at all.

3. 2 contradicts 1, and 1 fails.

The italicized part of this passage refers to the eyes being such that they can form images. But an image is a mental representation of nature, a picture in a mind: eyes don't have mental pictures in them, that's what minds are supposed to be doing, so the question would be, why do jellyfish have no brains but eyes that give rise to (mental) image formation? And, another question, is: How does it make 'decisions' about its reality (since, presumably, eyes prompt such activity as making decisions) from the eye information without a brain? Where does the information from the eyes go if there is no brain? Similar questions exist for other creatures, such as the slime mold, which can navigate through maze, by the mathematically shortest distance possible, to reach the food on the other side, and all this is done by a creature with no brain.

4. Conclusion: not-1

Gallant's research would only apply to cases where televisually experiencing creatures have observable PVC activity. If there are televisually experiencing humans who do not have evidence of having a PVC or utilizing a PVC to copy imprints into the PVC from the eyes, then Gallant's research would not overturn premise 3 of the simulation theory argument, and Gallant's work is just part of the story and cinema of human simulated reality.

Furthermore, this objection that comes from Gallant's work is not as powerful as it first appears, for several reasons, one such would be that it is not an objection about *consciousness*, since Gallant's work is, rather, merely about *light* interacting with the body: first the retina, and then later the PVC. If light patterns are imprinted in the retina, to discover that they are imprinted in an area of the brain is not only not surprising, but quite expected. But to go the next step, and to describe how these light imprints in the meat of the human brain lead to self-aware digital picture-screen experiencing, flushed with feelings, higher order capacities to do higher-order mathematics, and so forth, is quite a departure from mere light-imprinting in the retina and then being copied into the brain.

The Thought Implantation Arguments

From the simulation theory argument, as well as from copious evidence from other chapters in this book, we can arrive at further, powerful inferences about simulation theory. Firstly, I will present an argument which shows that conscious mindscreen content can only be *implanted* by another mind, not perceived-and-processed in a representational scenario.

Consider the following _reductio ad absurdum_:

1. Not-R

2. Since any ME in M_p is not caused by externality via R, then any ME is caused by another mental entity, ME*.

3. But ME* would require ME**, and so on, ad infinitum.

4. If any ME is created by another, ME*, a vicious regress ensues.

5. CONCLUSION: Any ME cannot be created by any other, non-identical ME^{n*}.

R stands for realism, ME stands for mental entity, M_p for mindprime[85].

Here is the argument, writing out the terms fully:

1. Conclusion of the simulation theory argument: consciousness is a simulation, not an apprehension of an externality.

2. Any mental content or mental entity does not come from any external reality, such as an external physical reality, so perhaps the mentation is caused by other mentation: one mental entity in one's mind (of any sort) can be the cause of, the reason for, any other mental entity that it appears to be possibly linked to in one's mind.

3. If one mental entity causes another, then another mental entity must cause the first, and another one causing the initial one, and so on, to infinity.

4. There is never a first step to the chain of mental entities causing one another, wherein there can't be any regress in the first place.

---

[85] Use mindprime to denote your mind, so when you are referring to your own mind, you are referring to mindprime.

5. CONCLUSION: no mental entity of any sort can cause any other mental entity to exist.

This is a quite straightforward vicious regress situation, which is somewhat similar to the well-known homunculus regress. We know realism (R) cannot account for mindscreen content, and the above argument also shows us that thoughts can't generate each other to account for their existence (any chunk of mindscreen content cannot create any other chunk of mindscreen content). So, what is left? If mental content is not caused by an externality, and if mental content is not generating and/or causing itself, then it would appear that *mental content and mental entities (MEs) must be implanted into the mindscreen*.

Now consider this argument, which uses the conclusion of the last argument:

1. Conclusion of previous argument, ~(ME➔ME*, for any ME or ME*).

2. Any ME, cannot create itself (lest that ME not have sufficient reason, unless the ME is a free-willed [supernatural] occurrence) .

3. Not-R.

4. CONCLUSION: Mindscreen consists of processes where MEs are *implanted* into M_p by something from $\sim M_p$, and $\sim R$.

If MEs cannot come from within the mindscreen, or be caused by copying or representing an externality that the mindscreen (believes it) is interacting with, then it seems that the conclusion we are left with is that another intelligence is composing the mindscreen content and placing it in mindscreens.

Premise 2 is important, in that it points out that there are two types of mental entities: implanted, and free-willed. For those who do not believe in free will, then there would only be one sort of ME, which is an implanted ME. Many are troubled by free-willed events since, ultimately, to be truly free and having no external cause, these are self-caused events, and possibly supernatural. It is most likely that merely the impetus, the "choice" (regardless of whatever "choice" could possibly mean, mechanically speaking), is all that the mindscreen does in the free will situation, and where after choice is made (in the rare occurrences that such free willed events happen), the implanter-simulator-creator creates (implants) the consequent mindscreen content. In a Christian perspective, this is not problematical, and is expected, since the human mindscreen is in God's image, where God is a creator of things _ex nihilo_, and thus a human can be expected to be such as well—such as in a creator of free-willed events ex nihilo and supernaturally. Regardless, if there are some self-caused, possibly supernatural, MEs, they would be free-willed, and seemingly not implanted MEs, at least at their impetus, wherein not _all_ of consciousness would be a computer simulation caused by external forces, since there would be a smattering of self-caused (free-willed) mindscreen events.

The word "implanted" here means that mental content is being placed into the mindscreen experiencing of M_p not by mapping its external environment via sensing (sense organs), nor by "one thought leading to anther", so to speak. Rather, a different means of MEs being placed into M_p exists. If MEs are not caused by an externality, nor by a mind causing its own content, the remaining option for how MEs could reside in M_p would appear to be that MEs are placed into M_p by another intelligence, such as the creator-simulator (or another mind or mental creature in simulation-space that has the capacity to do so[86]).

When one introspects to see the chaotic nature of mind, and how thoughts and feelings, viewed through introspection, come and go, where self is not the cause or deliberator of these MEs coming-and-going quickly in consciousness, it therein appears roughly as if thoughts and MEs are being implanted, and certainly do not appear as if one is choosing which MEs appear in mind, and introspection shows the mindscreen to take on the appearance of *an entity out of the control of the simulant*! This is a widely discussed mystery (though not a mystery for simulation theorists), such as with David Hume's well-known analysis of mind that led him to question the nature and existence of the self.

The ME Implanter Creator-Simulator is an Intelligence (and is God)

A reason for believing the aforementioned implantation scenario is due to the mindscreen content appearing to derive from another intelligence. Consider the following argument:

1. Conclusion of previous argument (Mindscreen consists of processes where MEs are *implanted* into M_p by something from $\sim M_p$, and $\sim R$).

---

[86] It does not seem that there could be another such implanter-mind or mindscreen *within* the simulation, since it, too, would have implanted consciousness (a simulated mindscreen), wherein the originator of the simulation, the creator-simulator, is the cause of the MEs for both M_p, and any other mind in the simulation that could be believed to be an implanter. In simpler terms, there can only be implanters outside of the simulation, and whom have control and capacity to implant MEs into M_p.

2. Collections of MEs that compose a mindscreen in M_p are not generated by copying (representing) the organized patterns from the content of a supposed externality.

3. If mindscreen content is not a facsimile, then it must be constructed, built, fabricated, more analogous to an artist creating a landscape than a copy-machine creating a landscape.

4. Collections of MEs that compose a mindscreen in M_p have organization, arrangement, which can only be positioned (strategically implanted) by an entity that can plan the construction of the mindscreen MEs.

5. CONCLUSION: The implanter of the MEs in M_p exhibits intelligence.

The implanter (creator-simulator) contains qualities possibly parallel to a computer programmer. The arguments given in this section appear to prove there is an implanter of MEs, and that would be a disproof of solipsism. That may not be a concern to many of the readers of this book, but a simple and powerful disproof of solipsism has not existed hitherto, and is something philosophers have been concerned with for some time. Further, just by directly knowing that M_p exists (which is irrefutable information), we can use that information to prove that a creator-simulator exists. This is roughly identical to saying that just by knowing M_p exists, one can know that God exists.

Reality Involves Other Mindscreen Simulants Not Identical to M_p

And since we know with logical certainty that a being describable as a creator-God has created M_p, one's mindscreen, and continues to create it at all moments, the Biblical message is that we are to exist in faith with other believers, and so, as described in Chapter 7 above, we know that the other persons we interact with in the simulation are other minds that are also having mindscreen experience, of you, and you interact in the simulation. And the following argument emerges:

1. This book proves the Bible is correct and YHVH is Lord-God.
2. If the Bible is correct, then we have genuine-and-real experience with other humans, in order to worship God.
3. Therefore, the other simulants we encounter in our daily life are also mindscreen simulations, just as you are, and you are having real experience of each other in your worlds (simulations) together.

The point of our existence, the meaning of life, is to have desimluation experience in Christ—this is my definition of worship. Further, since love is something *between* beings, not for a single being. A single could only love itself, which is narcissism, a type of misery.[87] Love is shared across beings, so the nature of the creator-God is to love and be loved, and God created our simulated existences together in order to generate yet more love, which the creator-Simulator would be interested in. For these reasons, it would appear to be inductively conclusive that other beings we are interacting with

---

[87] Interestingly, this is actually a reason why God is a One that is a Trinity: love is outer-directed ,and God can only be, in Himself, an interloving being, loving Himself as Other and as Self, in perfect lovingness.

in our simulated mindscreen experience are the body-suits, the simulation guises, of other mindscreen activity in the simulation, and they are not mindless apparitions or beings with no mental content, with only the _appearance_ of having mental content. In simpler terms, human simulants may be _actually_ interacting via shared simulation experience, where picture-screen feeling-infused realities of mindscreen simulants mix, to some degree.

Works Cited

Grupp, Jeff, 2019, March 17, 2019, "God IS EVERYWHERE, Sermon, Pastor Jeff Grupp, 3-17-19", YouTube Channel: Praise and Love, URL: https://www.youtube.com/watch?v=PXXKEXg--XA.

Grupp, Jeff, 2018a, Dec. 31, "Fullness Calvinism: Expanding Calvinist Theology to Resolve Big Theological Puzzles", YouTube Channel: Praise and Love, URL: https://www.youtube.com/watch?v=-LhIi8ZhjWM.

Grupp, Jeff, 2018b, "God's Pre-Election Knowledge of the Soul: A New Interpretation of Biblical Election and Predestination Showing Why God Only Chose Some Rather Than All," in _Theologic: Revelation, Calvinism, Surrender, Nothingness_, Kalamazoo: Praise and Love Church, (print copy available from Lulu books), pages 5-33.

Grupp, Jeff, 2018d, "Sin, Nothingness, the Liar Paradox, and the Contamination of Creation," in _Theologic: Revelation, Calvinism, Surrender, Nothingness_, Kalamazoo: Praise and Love Church, pages 32-54 print copy available at Lulu Books.

Grupp, Jeffrey, 2013, "Physical Reality is a Computer Simulation," University of Michigan – Dearborn, Humanities Winter Semester Colloquium Lecture, April 10, 2013, University of Michigan-Dearborn, CASL Room 1030, 3 pm.

Grupp, Jeffrey, 2006a, "Mereological Nihilism: Quantum Atomism, and the Impossibility of Material Constitution," *Axiomathes: An International Journal in Ontology and Cognitive Systems*, Vol. 16, No. 3, pp. 245-386.

Grupp, Jeffrey, 2006b, "Blob Theory: N-adic Properties Do Not Exist," *Sorites*, Vol. 17, pp. 104-131.

Grupp, Jeffrey, 2005a, "The R-Theory of Time, or Replacement Presentism: The Buddhist Philosophy of Time," *The Indian International Journal of Buddhist Studies* (IIJBS), No. 6, 2005, pp. 51-122.

Grupp, Jeffrey, 2005b, "The Impossibility of Temporal Relations Between Non-Identical Times: New Arguments for Presentism," *Disputatio: International Journal of Philosophy*, Vol. 1, No. 18, May 2005, pp. 91-125.

Grupp, Jeffrey, 2005c, "The Impossibility of Relations Between Non-Collocated Spatial Objects and Non-Identical Topological Spaces," *Axiomathes: An International Journal in Ontology and Cognitive Systems*, Vol. 15, No. 1, pp. 85-141(57).

Krotke, Wolf, 2005, *Sin and Nothingness in the Theology of Karl Barth*, Princeton: Princeton Theological Seminary.

Lorber, John, 1980, "Is Your Brain Really Necessary?", *Science*, Vol 210. 12. December. P. 1232-1234

Index